D0421926

THE HOUSE OF
PURPLE
HEARTS

THE HOUSE OF PURPLE HEARTS

STORIES OF
VIETNAM VETS
WHO FIND
THEIR WAY
BACK

PAUL SOLOTAROFF

HarperCollins*Publishers*

THE HOUSE OF PURPLE HEARTS. Copyright © 1995 by Paul Solotaroff. All rights reserved. Printed in the United States of America. No part of this book may be used or reproduced in any manner whatsoever without written permission except in the case of brief quotations embodied in critical articles and reviews. For information, address HarperCollins Publishers, Inc., 10 East 53rd Street, New York, NY 10022.

HarperCollins books may be purchased for educational, business, or sales promotional use. For information please write: Special Markets Department, HarperCollins Publishers, Inc., 10 East 53rd Street, New York, NY 10022.

FIRST EDITION

Designed by Nancy Singer

Library of Congress Cataloging-in-Publication Data

Solotaroff, Paul.
     The house of purple hearts : stories of Vietnam vets who find their way back / Paul Solotaroff.
     p.   cm.
     ISBN 0-06-017076-X
     1. New England Shelter for Homeless Vets. 2. Homeless veterans—Services for—Massachusetts—Boston. 3. Veterans, Disabled—Rehabilitation—Massachusetts—Boston. 4. Vietnamese Conflict, 1961–1975—Veterans. I. Title.
     UB384.A2S65   1995
     362.868'0973—dc20   95-6907

95 96 97 98 99 ❖/RRD 10 9 8 7 6 5 4 3 2 1

For my mother and father

I feel like a hitchhiker caught in a hailstorm on a
Texas highway. I can't run. I can't hide. And I can't
make it stop.

—Lyndon Baines Johnson

But Love has pitched his mansion in
The place of excrement;
For nothing can be sole or whole
That has not been rent.

—William Butler Yeats

FOREWORD

I think I'm fairly old and jaded, and nothing much impresses me, but I was impressed when I went to this shelter.

I first met Ken Smith when he was driving an ambulance. He called and said he didn't know me, but he'd like to talk.

He came by the house and told me that he was a combat veteran of Vietnam, that he saw his brother veterans sick, homeless, and dying every night on his rounds through Boston.

He was a member of a group of combat vets, and the group had decided to start a shelter.

They had an idea, the idea was to stage a play to earn enough money to get the shelter idea off the ground.

We staged an evening of songs, readings, drama, and poetry by and about service men and women.

Patti Wolff was the producer, I was the director, and the cast included Michael J. Fox, Kevin Bacon, Al Pacino, Don Ameche, Robert Prosky, Georg Stanford Brown, William Macy, Chuck Stransky, The Emerald Society of the N.Y.P.D., Dennis Franz, Charles Haid, Donald Sutherland. . . .

It was the most important theatrical evening of my life—it was, to me, everything that an evening in the Theater should be—it united the community in an issue which concerned us all, it entertained, and, to use an overused word, it cleansed.

It cleansed because it *brought the hidden to light*.

Freud wrote that the resistance is the neurosis; that is, it is not the traumatic event which causes mental imbalance, but rather the energy required to *suppress* the memory/truth/fact of that event.

An injustice was done to servicemen returning from Vietnam, and that injustice was compounded daily by the country-as-a-whole.

We, as a society, wanted to forget Vietnam. But, to quote Freud again, the only way to forget is to remember.

And the evening, *Sketches of War,* was, to my mind, an act, on the part of the Community as a whole, of apology and welcome. Something suppressed had been brought-to-light, and we all felt it was a first step toward community healing.

My association with the vets, with Ken, and Peace, and Howard, and Dan, and Mark, ended with the evening. My friendship continued, but I had nothing further to do with them and their plans for a shelter.

A year or two passed, we would meet now and then socially, and Ken would say "Drop by the shelter; I think you'll be proud of it."

I resisted going. I look back, it's clear that I did not want to be disillusioned by what I thought I would find there.

But my friend Michael Meritt was in town. We'd been working together for about twenty years, since he'd come back from Vietnam. First in Chicago, and then on Broadway, and now in Boston, we'd been doing movies and plays together—me writing, directing, and him designing.

He was in town to design a play, and it was to be his last. He was dying from cancer which was most probably caused by exposure to Agent Orange.

I knew he was talking to Ken and the vets at the shelter

about his Vietnam experiences—Kenny told me, on the phone, that Michael was letting things go that he had kept inside for twenty years, that he, in the company of his fellow vets, was talking about the war for the first time, and that it was doing him good.

"By the way," Kenny said, "why don't you stop by the shelter?"

So, in the spirit of someone doing a disagreeable good deed, I went to the shelter.

I found a 10-story building in the heart of downtown Boston, clean, neat as a pin, staffed exclusively by veterans, many of them ex-homeless veterans.

I expected an air of helplessness, and found, instead, a purpose.

The purpose of the shelter was to restore the veterans to society—*not* to warehouse them, *not* to rejuvenate them for the streets, but to put them back where they belong; and everything in the shelter, from the first greeting on, was directed to that end. And it was working.

I was stunned.

I thought of Theodore Herzl and the Dreyfus trial. In 1895 Herzl, a Viennese Jew, went to Paris as a reporter to cover the trial of Dreyfus, a French captain of artillery wrongly accused of espionage.

Dreyfus was railroaded and sent to Devil's Island, in a blatant instance of anti-Semitism.

Herzl went home to Vienna and began planning a Jewish State.

Most people he met told him he was wasting his time with a dream, and he responded, "If you will it, it is not a dream."

With love, to all the vets at the shelter,

David Mamet
Boston
13 January 1995

ACKNOWLEDGMENTS

As a writer of passions who happens to write journalism, I have set myself a pledge: to give names and faces to the nameless and faceless, and tell the stories of people without a voice to tell their own. My subjects are those who are strangled by silence, whose suffering is compounded for being made to keep mum. If there is anything I know and honor on this planet, it is the power of dire necessity: the story that absolutely needs to be told, the pain that needs to be tended.

For twenty-five years, the men in this book have suffered in terrible silence. They have lived under our noses but far out of earshot, exiles on Main Street America. It has cost us some peace not to hear about their war, because the very least we owed them was a hearing. Certainly, it would have grieved us to listen to their stories, but just as certainly it has grieved us *not* to, living instead with a neuralgia of shame, and consciences much stricken for having forsaken our soldiers. Twenty years after the fall of Saigon, it is time now for *all* of us to face the music, to grit our teeth bravely and bear the pain together. For too long, Vietnam veterans have had to bear it alone, and been crushed as much by our seeming indifference as by the weight of what they saw in the jungle.

A word or two about the pages to follow. I have altered or withheld the last names of a few of the vets, in the interest of legal discretion. Every man who told his story wanted his name attached to it, but where children or an ex-wife were thereby implicated, it was necessary to take this precaution. Second, because only men are treated at the New England Shelter for Homeless Veterans, I was unable to tell the story of any of the women who served in-country. I expect the narratives of those brave souls who staffed the evacs and operating rooms are as compelling as anything the men have to relate; sadly, their anguish has been virtually ignored, but for a piece in the *New York Times Magazine*.

This book could not have been written without the help of Ken Smith, who, on a red-hot mission to have the story of his brothers told, threw the doors and resources of his huge shelter open to me. So, too, with his partners Mark Helberg and Peace Foxx, who put themselves endlessly at my disposal, and made it their business that I got the story right. No less vast is my gratitude to Leslie Lightfoot, who nervously let me into her office during treatment, then gave unstintingly of her heart and her smarts. Ditto George Mendoza, the marvelous PTSD director, who suffered me to sit in on his combat support group, an evening I will never forget. Would that it were possible to clone Lightfoot and Mendoza and unleash them on the streets. An elite strike force of their kind would all but eradicate veteran homelessness, our "stateside MIAs," as Ken Smith calls them.

I owe a different kind of debt to Terry Karten, the editor I've been waiting for half my life. Thanks are due also to Craig Nelson, who instantly saw there was a book here and wasted no time acquiring it; to my father, Ted Solotaroff, whose literary restraint is my ballast; and to Elaine Stillerman, whose vivacity is the wind in my sails.

On behalf of Ken Smith, Mark Helberg, and Peace Foxx, I want to pay special acknowledgment to David Mamet, without whose early and frequent generosity this shelter would not exist. "David didn't know us from China, but he made our dream happen," says Smith. "There isn't a better friend anywhere to homeless vets than him." Adds Helberg, "Out of gratitude, I gave David my Purple Heart, a gift from one warrior to another."

And last, I want to thank the men of the shelter's combat support group, who gave it all up to me and held nothing back. That was no small gift; your story was the last thing you had. And so, with love and honor, I commit your story to the agency of the outgoing wind.

THE HOUSE OF
PURPLE
HEARTS

CHAPTER ONE

TWO YEARS AGO, ON ONE OF THOSE DAZZLING FALL days with which the city of Los Angeles is so profligately favored, I drove over to Venice Beach with a couple of hours on my hands. Wandering at my leisure among the sun-drunk tourists and shirtless surf boys tanned the color of toast, another day closer to acute melanoma, I began to notice a sprawl of sad, ragged men on the grass beside the boardwalk. Bundled in the shapeless, three-layer miscellany that is the year-round uniform of the homeless, they were distinctive nonetheless for what else they had on: jungle hats busy with pins and badges, olive-drab jackets bearing campaign patches, and T-shirts trumpeting THE 82ND AIR-BORNE: DEATH FROM ABOVE, MOTHERFUCKER.

Intrigued, I sat down on a dirty blanket with several of them, and discovered that here, on the contiguous sands of Venice and Santa Monica, sat two company-size elements of Vietnam veterans. Some of them were snowbirds, just in from parts elsewhere, one step ahead of the downbearing winter. Others had been here as long as twenty years, and set up crude hootches in the brown hills of Malibu, a kind of small, deep-growth Da Nang. Whatever their provenance, though, most of these two hundred men were *combat* vets, the decorated heroes of Hue and Khe Sahn, with the discharge papers to prove it.

Over the next two weeks, I spoke at length with several dozen of them about the cops who ambushed them at four in the morning, throwing their wallets and bedrolls into a Dumpster before hauling them off to jail; about the Crips and *cholos* who roamed the streets in ratpacks, looking for a vet with a General Relief check in his pocket; about the bilious damp that blew in come November, encasing them like a body bag through the middle of March. But mostly, these men talked to me about Vietnam, or, rather, talked *through* me to themselves in stunned recitation about the horror that had stopped them dead two decades ago, and detained them ever since in some POW camp of the soul.

By day, heavily anesthetized on booze and dope, they wandered around the spectacular wreckage of their past, surveying it with the dispassion of insurance adjusters. But at night, after the freak show of the boardwalk shut down and the idiot children of the sixties had gone home to braid their hair, the grief and the terror rolled in like thunder. There was Roy, born and raised to be a Chicago bluesman but transformed by the Army into a Special Forces assassin, who couldn't stop telling me about that day near Da Nang when a noise spun him around to see his best friend holding what looked like an octopus; it was, instead, his small intestine, blown half out of him by a VC hang mine. Hours later, after the kid had bled to death in his arms, Roy stumbled into the latrine and found bits of his buddy's skin all over his flak jacket. There was Black Scotty, who'd lost a third of the men in his company, and who by the end of his tour was so beset with grief that he couldn't sleep without a spike of heroin. And there was White Scotty, with his spectral gaze, ceaselessly haunted by what he and his squadron had done aboard their P-3 bomber over Haiphong Harbor, blowing up women and children on creaky rafts as they ferried ammunition down the coast.

In the course of reporting what became a long article for *Vanity Fair*, I learned that there were at least half a million veterans on the streets of America, about a third of them Vietnam vets. Put another way, more than twice as many survivors of that war were dying of dope and hypothermia here as had been killed in Southeast Asia. Furthermore, almost a million soldiers had come back from Vietnam with the disastrous psychic affliction called Post-Traumatic Stress Disorder, a progressive illness whose early symptoms (depression, withdrawal, sleeplessness) generally go undiagnosed, and whose later eruptions (psychosis, manic violence, suicide) devastate both the afflicted and their families. In the introduction to the latest edition of his landmark book, *Home from the War*, Robert Jay Litton notes that Vietnam veterans with PTSD are five times likelier to be unemployed than those without it, and up to six times likelier to have abused drugs and alcohol. Fully half, moreover, have been arrested or put in jail at least once since their return from Vietnam.

Fifteen years ago, PTSD was barely a blip on the screen, charting up only when some vet in full jungle gear shot himself on the steps of City Hall, or plowed his pickup through the doors of a VA hospital that had summarily discharged him. But in the late seventies and early eighties, a vast number of Vietnam vets in their middle thirties suddenly broke down and found themselves out on the street, leaving behind them, in their freefall into isolated ruin, mortgages and car payments, and heartbroken families. Certainly, the collapse of the economy had some part in this, turning the heat up on men already verging on psychic flame-out. The deeper reason, however, said the vets on the beach, was that the rage, grief, and horror they'd been sitting on since the war had finally outstripped their power to suppress it, and no amount of self-medication was going to stave it off another minute.

"The beer and the dope, they cooled me out for a while, just like back in the 'Nam," said Black Scotty. "But the more I kept feedin' it, the bigger the monster, till one day I woke up lookin' at King Kong."

One night, shortly after my arrival in Venice, I found Black Scotty weeping in a blue pagoda under a moon the color of shark's teeth. It was almost ten o'clock and everyone else had headed out, trudging the three hundred yards over to the Santa Monica side, where the cops deigned to let them sleep on the beach. For the second night running, however, Black Scotty could not lie down; the memories were flame-stitched to the inside of his eyelids.

"Alla them kids dead, man, just like that, because the C.O., who I shoulda killed when I had the chance to, made us sit up at attention, and everyone knows you ain't s'posed ta sit up in 'Nam," he sobbed. "The VC was in the trees, we coulda reached out and touched 'em but we couldn't see 'em and they sprayed the tent and all them damn boys died. I *knew* better, I had two tours over there. I tried to tell 'em, 'Y'all stay down,' but the C.O. gave orders, and they sat up and shots busted and . . ."

He stopped, the sentence lodging like a bone in his throat. He looked up in torment, raking his nails across his chest, as if trying to rip out his broken heart. "I shoulda *shot* the motherfucker, I shoulda left him in the Dumpster. I told him, 'Bitch, don't even *try* to go to sleep tonight. . . .'"

Another round of sobs, still more racking than the last. I

knelt there, spinning my wheels, wondering how to begin to help him. He'd done two tours of nightmare duty in 'Nam, and none of it was supposed to have happened. A proud kid from a dirt shack family in south Florida, he'd had a year of junior college under his belt and a future in computer programming when he got conned by a Marine recruiter. The recruiter told him that if he came off his college deferment, they'd pay for his education and stash him in Officer Candidate School. Instead, they shipped him out ASAP to Da Nang, a grunt in the middle of the Tet Offensive. Thereafter, he and what remained of his unit were dispatched to wherever the fighting was fiercest: Quang Tri, Pleiku, Chu Lai, Happy Valley. Somehow, he came out of it with all his limbs intact, but lost more buddies than he could begin to register, and by the time he made it back to his mother in Tampa, he'd developed what he called an "either-or" addiction to heroin—"Either I got high, or someone was gonna die."

"Scotty," I pressed him, as I had for half an hour, "why don't you try taking your medication now?"

Sitting in his frayed duffel bag was a bottle of Elavil, and a second psychotropic that he couldn't pronounce. But Black Scotty, who was generally deemed the steadiest of the Venice vets, and who spent most of his time baby-sitting the "51/50's" (military slang for out-and-out nutjobs), wouldn't hear of it. The pills brought on "The Dream," he said, and The Dream was about to drive him cold out of his mind.

"Always the same one, over and over—I can't shake it no kinda way," he croaked. "I'm in the bush on search-and-destroy and a sniper starts shootin' at us, walkin' it in closer and closer. Quick, I roll thataway, behind a banana tree, but there's a gook standin' over me with a muzzle in my face. I roll the other way, behind another tree, and there's a gook

5

there, *too*. Every damn where I roll, there's a gook waitin' on me, ready to squeeze one off. I wake up screaming and my heart goin' *BOOM!* like a straight-up heart attack, and you know what? I wish it *would*. I'm tired a' sittin' here, watchin' and waitin'. I just wanna go to sleep and not wake up no more. . . ."

"THE HYPERVIGILANCE HE'S DESCRIBING, AND the suicidality—I see both things over and over in treatment," says Dr. Jonathan Shay, an eminent VA psychiatrist who for fifteen years has been treating PTSD in Vietnam veterans, and whose book on the subject, *Achilles in Vietnam*, was published to much acclaim last year. "A lot of these men have lost all sovereignty over mental functions, and can be invaded at any second by the utmost horror. Like concentration camp survivors, their bodies are living in a parallel reality that has nothing to do with real-time experience. One moment, a vet can be numb and withdrawn, the next moment screaming in combat hysteria, his pulse rate going at 120 a minute.

"And even the vets without full-blown flashbacks as such have little or no control over memories and feelings. Not only can they not trust someone else's authority—after the way they saw authority abused in Vietnam—but they can't even begin to trust their own. That's as close to a global injury as you get."

Jim Dwyer, a former Marine who is now the director of the Vietnam Vets Liaison Unit at the VA Medical Center in West Los Angeles, concurs. "The thing that makes PTSD so difficult to treat—pardon me, *one* of the things that makes it so difficult to treat—is that mayhem done to their basic sense of trust. I mean, had these guys done even half the things they were told to over there, they'd have come home, most of them, in body bags. Why should they invest now in someone like me, even though I'm a Vietnam combat vet myself and have been fighting on their behalf since 1975?"

No less obdurate than their mistrust, says Dwyer, is the vets' intransigent guilt. "What we see time and again in these men is the unconscious wish to be punished. Their sense of self is so badly damaged by having not done something, or in the case of atrocity guilt, about having done too much. We had a guy here who went out and killed himself one day when he suddenly remembered, after years of blocking it, that he'd called in the wrong coordinates in the field and wiped out four of his buddies. That tragedy taught us to go *very* slowly with these guys, to help them unwrap [their memories] with extreme caution. And we won't even attempt intensive therapy until we've got them at least six weeks clean and sober. Substance abuse and trauma tend to marry each other, which may be the biggest single obstacle to getting them to come in—they're terrified of what's going to happen once they stop medicating themselves."

Dwyer's right; at night, you can feel the panic build on the boardwalk, as the dope and the money run low. Beneath palm trees that hulk like hooded thugs, their fat crowns obfuscating the streetlights, vets cluster together not for warmth or fraternity but for the sake of group survival. The night before I arrived on the beach, the Shoreline Crips had barreled through, swinging bats and slashing pockets with their double-ohs and box-cutters. Up the way a bit, a vet named Wolfie had been stabbed, and another, named Curtis, beat down with a brick.

But for all the menace and affliction of the beach, the vets to a man told me they felt safer there than they did in the hands of the VA. Stories are elicited up and down the boardwalk about the despotic whims of VA doctors, and the bedlam misery of the wards they preside over. In the early eighties, while he was still holding on by the skin of his teeth to a job, Black Scotty went to the Oakland VA in dire need of PTSD treatment; instead, they diagnosed him as paranoid schizophrenic and committed him to six months in the locked ward upstairs. At the other end of the country, a vet named Chuck was strapped down to a cot and robotized on megadoses of Haldol and Thorazine.

Many forests could be denuded documenting the VA's derelictions, among them its failure to recognize PTSD until 1979, when the mental health community had to drag it, kicking and screaming, into the second half of the twentieth century, and its ruthless adherence to a Civil War statute that prevented vets from retaining lawyers to sue for benefits. But, as will be made plain in the pages to follow, nothing tops its wide-ranging, clinical maltreatment of men whose only offense was to have served in an unpopular war.

To be sure, there have always been and will continue to be heroes on the VA's staff of 200,000, people like Shay and Dwyer who have quietly made their lives into a kind of mission on behalf of these men. But for every Shay or Dwyer, there seems to have been three of Robert Nimmo, the former VA Secretary who forever endeared himself to 'Nam vets by likening Agent Orange to teenage acne, and pooh-poohed PTSD as if it were some sort of insurance scam.

"In '77 and '78, when the streets were starting to fill up with Vietnam vets, we went to the VA and *begged* them to move on this—and, instead, had the door slammed hard in our face," says Michael Blecker, a former Bronze Star winner in the 101st Airborne who, as the founding director of Swords to Plowshares in San Francisco, was in at the birth of what has become a national coalition of Vietnam veteran advocates. "To be fair, the whole country was in denial at the time, acting like the war had never happened. But the VA was supposed to have been our *advocate*, not our adversary, and for fifteen years did everything in its power to screw us from top to bottom."

"What you've had until very recently was a VA run by and for World War II vets, whose attitude was, 'We won *our* war and you lost yours, so we don't owe you cowards and baby-killers anything,'" says Ralph Cooper, executive director of the Veterans Benefits Clearinghouse and a key player in the twenty-year, grass-roots struggle to secure adequate treatment for Vietnam vets. "Now, the good news is that we're finally starting to see some new faces over there, people like Jesse Brown and Smith Jenkins who are busting their tails to help vets get their claims moved along. But the bad news is that so many guys out there have just flat given up, been abused to the point where they don't care anymore and are living like animals in the wild. Ten years ago, with any help from the VA, we probably could've saved most of them. Now, I just don't know."

A MONTH AFTER MY LAST NIGHT ON THE BEACH in Venice, Roy called me, collect, from what sounded like the bottom of the ocean. Black Scotty and White Scotty had been collared on separate charges, and without them for backup, he'd been bum-rushed by a gang of skinheads. "I can't deal no more, man, I'm goin' back up into the hills. I was safer in Da Nang than I am out here."

His hurt was distinct over the *wah-wah* of phone static. Many of the men he'd served with in Da Nang had died there, and I knew some little of what it had cost him to come home alive: the excruciating break with his family in

Chicago, who lived in terror of his vagrant rages, and his total psychic collapse in 1985, when for six months he couldn't feed himself or leave the house. No, Da Nang hadn't killed him but had so poisoned his soul that he spent most nights wishing he *had* died.

He gave me a message to pass on to either Scotty and gallantly refrained from hitting me up for money. But in the gathering howl of interference on the line, I heard him working his way up to another request. "Yo, are you gonna be talkin' to any of the brass at the VA?"

Yes, I said, I would.

"Well, could you ask 'em something for me? See, they gave amnesty to all the ones that ran away to Canada. In '77, President Carter told 'em all to come on home and everything'd be forgiven, and it was. What I wanna know is, when will *we* be forgiven? We didn't *try* to lose that war; we tried to serve our country. When can *we* come home?"

IF YOU WRITE AT LENGTH, AS I DO, ABOUT THE carnage of L.A.'s gang wars, or about the brutal sex trade of homeless children in New York, you come around fairly quickly to the dismal view that there are pockets of misery so entrenched in this country that no prospect of rescue is imaginable. It is as though the earth has caved in on certain classes of people, burying them beneath the rubble of our cumbrous contempt and removing them from public view. So I'd begun to construe the plight of Vietnam veterans, abandoned and betrayed by many VA clinicians and generally regarded even by private therapists as largely untreatable.

"The sad truth is, most of these men never get any better, no matter how much goodwill you bear them," said one New York psychiatrist well known for his work with trauma victims. "The damage is too vast, and by now, pretty much armor-clad. You're dealing not with one or two buried episodes [of horror] but with dozens stacked up on top of one another. Then, you factor in the effects of the addictions and VA drugs, and all the postwar tumult they're carrying around—the broken marriages, the kids they've abused or left behind—I mean, it's a stacked deck even if they're in a position to do long-term work with you, and they almost never are. The most I usually manage is to fine-tune their medications—and hope that they've got the wherewithal to go on taking them."

But then, near the end of two months' research, I stumbled upon a light in all this darkness. Early on, I'd heard from advocates like Blecker that ad hoc veterans' groups had sprung up around the country, essentially self-help outfits run by and for Vietnam vets. I was moved by the thought of eight or ten men huddled together in some church cellar, hacking away at the shared tendrils of rage and sadness, but discounted the notion as sadly insufficient to the problem. I later learned, however, that several of these operations had evolved into full-service clinics, providing shelter and detox and soup-to-nuts therapy for thousands of afflicted vets. Notable among them is the aforementioned Swords to Plowshares in San Francisco—which began life in two rooms above the Tenderloin YMCA and is now a million-dollar, forty-bed facility in the Mission—and the Vietnam Veterans of San Diego, whose staff of thirty-six treats homeless veterans right across the street from the Marine Corps Recruitment Depot.

But by far the biggest and most impressive program in the country is the New England Shelter for Homeless Veterans, an extraordinary, $5-million-a-year operation that houses and rehabs 1,500 men a year. It was founded in 1989 by three combat vets—Ken Smith, Mark Helberg, and Peace Foxx—who, with their zealous staff of 130, have succeeded where the VA has failed utterly: in ferrying sick and strung-out vets from the streets and converting most of them into proud, sober, independent taxpayers.

To do so, Smith et al. have essentially created a humane version of the Army. Under stringent security and martial discipline, all the necessities of the 350 residents are met: three hot meals a day, a clean bed (not a cot), several changes of new clothes, and ready medical attention. Instead of military maneuvers, however, the men march off to a job each morning, or to a college-prep course, or computer training. In the afternoon, they report not to a buck sergeant but to a drug counselor, with whom they repeal the addictions many of them contracted in the service. And for those men at the heart of this rabid mission—the 25 percent who are Vietnam combat vets with PTSD—there is extensive and stunningly successful therapy on site, and the prospect of closure after twenty years in hell.

"The Army makes men; we *remake* them," says Smith, who without a college degree or a dime to his name talked Congress into handing him the keys to an abandoned hospital in the heart of downtown Boston, and in five years has transformed it into a monolith of powers and services. In the worst recession in fifty years and under appalling physical conditions—all ten floors of the building were uninhabitable when he took possession—Smith and his partners have ceaselessly grown the project. There is an employment office on the mezzanine that places one hundred vets a month in high-paying jobs, and funnels hundreds more into the VA's Compensated Work Program, where vets earn money while being retooled for new careers. Next door, in the housing office, a staff of three locates an apartment for every man who completes the program, browbeating realtors into renting to men who have generally been homeless for years. On the first floor, a team of third-year law students works to clear up outstanding warrants for the vets and to represent those with PTSD in their disability cases before the VA. After two decades of being denied compensation for their illness, many of these men have recently won substantial pensions, and a measure of vindication long since due them.

"You want to know what PTSD is all about?" grunts Smith, who combines the peremptory swagger of a general with the rage of a fucked-over grunt. "It's about *injustice*, a burning anger in the pit of your stomach. Every man here, when he was called to duty, put his life on the line for his goddamned country, and in return got raped and shit on for his trouble. Everything that we've done here, every dollar we've raised, is to see that amends are finally made to these guys, and that they've got whatever they need to take back their lives."

With great pride, he shows off the new optometry clinic, and the sleek wall of showers Al Pacino wrote a check for on his last trip through the shelter. Before Smith is anything, he is a master salesman, and the fruits of his suasion are everywhere: the tens of thousands of dollars of brand-new clothing donated by local department stores, which hangs on the racks of his basement supply room and is handed out to residents free of charge; the twenty IBM desktops given to the second-floor computer school, which graduates a class of thirty every three months to waiting jobs in the insurance and banking industries; and the blueprint for sixty SRO apartments upstairs, to be built on a $4.2 million grant from HUD for vets too impaired to live on their own.

*   *   *

BUT FOR ALL THE LATE IMPROVEMENTS AND amenities at the shelter, the protocol here is brutally plain: get in, get sober, get a job, get out. This isn't some soft asylum with pastel walls and pink-cheeked nurses who sluice the air. This is tough-love triage, boot camp for broken souls, and the Parris Island discipline starts at the front door. Walk in and one of three guards stops you and pats you down, whether you're a sailor looking for a flop or the grandstanding Congressman from the Third District. And if, like most of the men who come in here for the first time, you're drunk or stoned or both, you're instantly confronted with the terms of the place: commit now to a stint in detox, and to turning your life around, or get the hell out and make room for the guy behind you.

"I've got a steady waiting list of one hundred vets to get in here, so if you want to play games, go do it someplace else," says Smith. "And if you need a little help making up your mind, we've got a memorial wall over there with the names of the guys who ate it. Hero soldiers who died like rats in the gutter from ODs and hypothermia."

The house rules are numerous, and vigorously enforced: no booze, no drugs, no weapons, no violence, no theft, no untidiness, no backtalk—no exceptions. Furthermore, everybody works here, virtually from the day he's assigned a bed. If, by the end of your third week, you haven't found a job or refused the one assigned you, you're summarily asked to leave the premises.

"Every man in this place has at least one thing going for him—that pride he felt the day he left boot camp a soldier," says Smith. "I appeal to that pride, I beat 'em over the head with discipline; it's the other half of the therapeutic equation here. [Psychological] treatment is well and good, but it doesn't count for much without a job. For a vet who's been on the street, nothing builds back self-esteem like watching his bank account grow. That's why every week, I make each guy deduct half of whatever he earns and bank it in a high-yield money market account. That way, by the end of their stay here, each man has a stake of at least three or four grand that he can put toward rent and a month's security.

"Now, understand, some of these guys will never leave. Some of 'em were so badly damaged in 'Nam, they'll be with me till the day they die. But the rest heal up and head out of here, and none of 'em hit the street without a job and an address. This isn't a recycling plant we're running; when you go, I don't want to see you back here again, unless it's to volunteer or show off pictures of your beautiful fiancée."

Not everyone is fast in love with Smith's drillmaster tack. Scarcely a day goes by without a vet taking me aside to bitch about Smith's bullying tone of address, or his peremptory decision to bar someone from the building. But the upshot of his bulldog stringency is that Smith is presiding over the safest and most functional shelter I have ever set foot in. The second-floor barracks gleam like spit-shined brass—the tile floors mopped to a fare-thee-well, the starched-sheet beds made as tight as trampolines. Even the cafeteria, which serves over 7,000 meals a week and is used as a day room by the dozens of vets unable to get a bed here, is conspicuous for its military sparkle. Leave a plate or an empty soda can behind on a table, and watch three vets come after you like you just spit on the flag.

In fact, the thing you're most struck by after a couple of days in this place is the audible hum of pride and community. What has been masterfully evoked in each of these crabbed, desolate men is a sense of brotherhood under siege, a rabid fraternity of the unloved and cast out. Vietnam vet or not, they curry strength from that open wound, and cleave to each other as if they were under constant incoming. The clinical staff of forty (many of whom began here as homeless vets) typically puts in ten-hour days, then drops by on the weekends to baby-sit the more delicate cases. A large volunteer force scrambles to do the scut work, running the mess hall and laundry room and trading sweat equity for the hundreds of tons of food donated by wholesale grocers. And whenever a 'Nam vet signs into the PTSD program upstairs, he is swept up in a round of backslaps and bear hugs, inducted bodily, as it were, into the tribe.

For most of these men, that ferocious embrace is their first moment of juncture in twenty years. In Vietnam vets, alienation is a vast, pathogenic thing, a dead connection to the rest of the sentient world. It began in the jungle as grief and horror, and congealed into a strangling silence back home, where the vets found it impossible to speak of Vietnam to anyone who hadn't been there. "I came home from the war all by myself, just me and forty caskets on the plane," recalls one vet. "Thirty hours later, I was back in Boston, running into all my old buddies in the square. They go, 'Hey, man, where the hell have *you* been?' I just looked at 'em and said, 'Ah, forget it, man. You wouldn't begin to understand.'"

Since the shelter first opened for business in 1990, the face of America has passed through its doors: teachers, welders, carpenters, chemists, truck drivers, linemen—you name it. All told, 4,000 men have remade their lives here, beneficiaries of the rough magic of sobriety and brother-love—and the ministrations of people like George Mendoza, the shelter's PTSD director. One after another, these haunted, death-hardened men, many of them carrying rapes and murders on their rap sheets, get weepy when talking about Mendoza, whom they've nicknamed Saint George the Dragon Slayer. They shake their heads, looking back on those early sessions with him, when they raged and sobbed like children in his arms, then came back an hour later with fresh horror to disgorge. This isn't the temperate therapy of Freud and Adler; this is a dig in a mass grave site, unearthing bodies and memories, and the stench of sulfur is everywhere.

"There are days when it's like the Tet invasion in here," says Mendoza, glancing over his shoulder at the gouge in his office wall, put there by a vet in a paroxysm of agony. "So much trauma, and it just keeps coming and coming— compound fractures of the heart and the spirit. That's why it's so important for the therapist to have been a warrior himself—to understand not just the special pain of being a warrior but to be able to deal with its intensity when it comes pouring out of them."

Most of the men Mendoza sees here had been treated elsewhere for PTSD, and grown into expensive, cynical consumers; one of them, in fact, had been admitted to VA hospitals in all fifty states and Puerto Rico, personally costing taxpayers something on the order of $3 million. These men glare bloody murder when you ask them about the VA, recalling the battle-ax contempt of its aging psychiatrists, and PTSD groups run by women social workers in their early and middle twenties.

"A total fucking nightmare over there," says Danny, a heavily decorated survivor of the siege of Khe Sanh, who has been homeless since 1975. "I kept reaching out and reaching out for help from the VA, and every time they'd tell me, 'There is no cure for PTSD,' or 'We can't help you, you're too severe for us.' Well, the day I met George, I knew they were lying to me. There was just immediate rapport there, big-time trust; I felt like I'd finally met someone who honestly cared. To this day, I consider the man my savior. He's a very special individual."

That Mendoza can connect so quickly with these men is a function both of empathy and shared experience. He is himself a combat veteran recovering from PTSD, a fact he conveys feelingly to the men in the very first session. "I tell them that even though it was a different war in a different country [the so-called Dirty War against the generals in Argentina]," says Mendoza, "I too know what it was like to be under fire at a young age, and to lose everything you have when the shooting's over—relatives, best friends, house, money. I even lost my beautiful country."

One step ahead of the death squads, Mendoza fled with his family to the United States in 1983, but was quickly felled in Boston by a savage depression. "I couldn't get out of bed for months and months; my two young boys had to go to work to support me. Finally, my wife found someone for me to talk to, a 'Nam combat vet researching the psychological consequences of war. I went to him, and it was like a revelation to me, discovering all these other men with spiritual injuries. Even so, it took me a long time to recover—at least two or three years to get back my self-esteem."

Thanks to the skills Mendoza has acquired in the decade since, training with PTSD pioneers like Dr. Edward Parson of the University of Massachusetts, most of his patients are substantially healed in less than half that time—and without the panoply of drugs that the VA pushes. Consider someone like Danny, who, despite a heavy regimen of sedatives and psychotropics, was by his own account "ballistic" when the VA discharged him here. In the eighteen years since he'd walked out on his wife and baby daughter and hopped a bus to Florida with fifty dollars in his pocket, this small, gaunt man with a face like a bruised fist had compiled an arrest record that would stretch from hell to Quang Tri. He'd blinded his wife in one eye with a Sunday punch, broken both hands repeatedly in barroom brawls, and been beaten into a coma by five cops outside Boston, whom he'd taken on in handcuffs.

Once a bright, ebullient kid with his heart set on becoming a lawyer, Danny had come back from the war so hateful that his family begged him to go in for a brain scan. What they didn't know, because he wouldn't tell them, was what he'd endured over there. A grunt in the notorious One-Nine Marines—dubbed the "Walking Dead" for their disastrous casualty rate—Danny had been stranded on a hill for seventy-seven days during the merciless siege of Khe Sanh. So withering was the mortar fire that pinned down his unit, no chopper would come in and dust off the wounded, condemning many of the men up there to bleed to death helplessly. And when at last Danny walked off Hill 861, skeletal from hunger and unbathed in three months, his C.O. ordered him on to hump the next hill, where, six hours later, he was shot by a VC sniper. Flown to a naval base in Japan, he awoke in horrible pain to find himself stranded on an amputee ward. At all hours of the day and night, the men around him emerged from morphine stupors to discover, anew, the loss of arms and legs.

"Some of 'em looked like home plate to me—all they were was just a chest and a head," murmurs Danny, his battered hands rattling like bone china in an earthquake. "I was havin' nightmares, everyone else there was havin' nightmares—even when they were wide awake—and when they'd come out of it and look down, they'd just scream and scream. Bein' there was worse than the 'Nam for me."

It went on like this without letup for Danny. Instead of

getting shipped home as promised by the doctors, he was sent back to his decimated unit in the jungle, where, in the three-alarm heat, his wounds opened and festered. Rushed to a hospital in Cam Ranh Bay with a 106-degree fever, he was packed in ice when a company of men was wheeled in, roasted by napalm. "I can still remember what they smelled like, one hundred guys burning up in the beds next to me," says Danny, who, when he was finally discharged from the service in 1969, had become a walking anthology of survivor guilt.

Small wonder, then, that by the time he came into the shelter in 1992, he'd made several serious bids to kill himself and had had last rites pronounced over him on three separate occasions. For twenty-three years, he'd been obliterating consciousness with sad declensions of pills and powder, and was drinking off his $800-a-month VA pension at the rate of a half-gallon a day. His parents lived in utter dread of him, and even his precious daughter, who alone had been spared his violence, begged and pleaded with him to stay away. "I love you, Daddy," she'd sob on the phone, "but please don't come around—I'm scared to death of you."

Says Danny, "When I first came to the shelter, I had so much hate and anger in me, I didn't give a fuck for nothing or no one—not my wife, my kid, my mother or my father. But George *listened*, I could speak to him for six hours straight—and this went on for like eighteen months. I've done a *lotta* work with him, believe me, recalling shit I'd been trying to numb out for twenty-five years—and most nights, I *still* wake up at three in the morning sometimes, the bed completely soaked like somebody threw a bucket of water on it.

"But, my God, so much has changed for me since I started with George," marvels Danny, who has been clean and sober for better than three years. "I see my daughter now on weekends, and talk to her twice a week on the phone," he says. "Last Friday night, in fact, we chatted till all hours like a coupla schoolkids, though afterward I got hit with big-time guilt. Why couldn't I have done the right thing and had a life with this kid, 'cause, you know, she's just so goddamn super—"

He breaks off, stanching the tears in his throat, then gathers himself with a breath. "Anyway, I've moved into a new complex in Charlestown, a luxury one-bedroom on the grounds of the old naval yard. For me, the ocean's a very special place—I grew up on fishing boats—and this place is right on the water, fifteen minutes from here by water taxi. And, thanks to George, I won a big [disability] case with Social Security, which, along with the upgrade in my VA pension, is gonna leave me pretty set for a while. For sure, I've still got a lotta issues left, and there's many a day I'm quite capable of murder. But for a long time, I said that if I could just have one year of happiness in my life, that's all I'd ever want from God—and between you, me, and the lamppost, I think it's gonna happen."

Before we part, I ask him what he's been given here that he didn't get at the VA. "*Hope*," he grunts, without so much as blinking. "As long as I'm willin' to come through that door sober, they're willin' to try to help me. That's what the Vietnam vet needs—not a handout, a hand *up*—and that's what this place gave me in spades."

WHAT FOLLOWS, THEN, IS THE STORY OF THIS remarkable place, as told first through the narrative of one of its founders, Ken Smith, then, sequentially, through the narratives of five of its clients, all of them Vietnam vets treated for severe PTSD. The five were chosen not because their stories were the most graphic or compelling, but, rather, because they were, in some way or other, the most representative, broadly reflecting the kinds of core experiences described by the hundreds of vets I interviewed. We begin with Jack, a former crew chief in Da Nang who, among other things, is haunted by his killing of an unarmed peasant, and conclude with Richie Haudel, the ex-recon trooper who chose solitary confinement over continued atrocities in the field, and who, at 50, is one of the most extraordinary men I have ever met.

But then, they are all extraordinary to me, every man of them. No one knows how many Vietnam vets have drunk themselves to death, or stuck a gun in their mouth on their mother's front lawn (the unconfirmable rumor, much repeated at the shelter, is that twice as many vets have committed suicide in America as were killed in Southeast Asia). It is no accident, however, that the vets under Smith's roof have survived. They are sad and they are bitter, but to a man, they are indomitable, determined to reclaim what's left of their lives from that war. In their courage and crude fraternity, you cannot help but be moved by them, and by their resolve to be defined not by the last twenty-five years, but the *next* twenty-five. In 1969, I was one of those kids throwing eggs at them, sighting a mile down my nose in know-nothing contempt. Today, I stand up, abashed and disabused, to say to Ken Smith and the proud men of 17 Court Street: Welcome home, friends, and forgive my not having said it sooner. Welcome home, after all these years, from the war.

Chapter Two

IT HADN'T RAINED TWICE IN SIX MONTHS IN DA Nang, and when the nine birds peeled out of Battalion that morning, the dirt they kicked up was as barbed as shrapnel. Squad leader Ken Smith, a bone-thin, bullet-faced mama's boy from Rhode Island, was packed into the second chopper with the first lieutenant and forward observer. Beneath his 60-pound rucksack and 12-pound flak jacket, he was already swamped and miserable in his profuse sweat, and in imminent danger of passing out cold. He and his crew had just come back from a ten-day mind-fuck in the bush, where they'd been fragged and outfoxed by a ghost contingent of the Cong. All told, he'd caught maybe a dozen hours sleep in the last week, and the only thing propping up his concrete eyelids now was the dead certainty that his great good luck was about to run out.

He'd been in-country for three months, give or take a week, and so far, was pitching a perfect game: no burns, no bullet holes, no buddies killed in action. Matters of personal health aside, however, everything else had been a horror show there. He'd enlisted in April under the fierce delusion that the great cause of liberty was at issue, that America had staked its might on behalf of a gallant and grateful republic. But in the gypsy slums outside U.S. base camps, South Vietnamese women glared at him with wildfire hatred, clutching their babies furtively, like satchel charges. And in the fighting holes they dug at night, high out of their minds on killer speed called Obesitol, Smith's hootchmates rhapsodized about burning the whole country down, and letting the dentists figure out who was VC and who was Friendly. This was no freedom fight, this was a cluster-fuck, he'd discovered, and what mattered now was staying awake until they sent him home. Fall asleep, and the night would blow his ass from here to Bien Hoa.

Looking out the doors of the deafening bird, he saw two choppers on either side of his in tight formation, and a couple of Cobras above them, along for extra muscle, their rocket pods glittering in the gunmetal dawn. It doesn't figure, Smith muttered. Why all this firepower for a chicken-shit detail? Hadn't the C.O. rousted them out at four in the morning to tell them he was sending them on a piece-of-ass operation: three days of baby-sitting some big artillery in a nearby valley, eating hot meals, slugging cold beer, and sleeping five klicks from Charlie? Obviously, *somebody* was lying to *somebody*, Smith seethed. Of all the thousand things he abominated about 'Nam, none burned him more than its bristling economy of lies. Except for the buddies that you partnered a hootch with, everybody else in this ripe, green hell liked to piss on your back and tell you it was raining.

Smith looked out the doors of the bird again and noticed they'd been going around in circles for fifteen minutes. *Now, what the fuck*, he snarled, bilious beyond words, when suddenly the nose of the starboard Cobra dipped, and *brrrrr-dddddddpppp!* went its cannons and mini-guns. "Hot fuckin' LZ!" screamed the right-door gunner, monkeying frantically with his balky M-60. Below them, the three Cobras swooped into the mouth of a valley, training their fire on the taller of two hills. Its flat, dun crown was roughly the circumference of a city rooftop, and on it could be made out two dozen or so specks scuttling like cockroaches to get to the sides of the hill, where the treeline would swallow them up. By now, all nine birds were fixed and focused, throwing a stupendous amount of ordnance at their targets: 20-mm rockets that carved out craters the size of sand traps, and mini-gun rounds that murdered the mustard blossoms at 1,100 per minute. In the command bird, descending, Smith's balls were in his throat. Forget those two dozen VC, they're meat, he told himself; worry about the two hundred more you *can't* see down there.

Scared savage as they hit the ground and rolled, the men of Delta Company tore things up with their M-16s, emptying at least a clip into every prostrate body, a carnival of overkill. Running by one of those bodies, Smith discerned the face of a small child, the top half of its head gone and its left leg severed, sitting neatly beside the hip socket as if awaiting reinsertion. Over the crackle of small-arms fire, Smith heard someone cry out for a medic, and sprinted toward a soldier who was tending two prone figures. Bending over them, Smith discovered that both were, again, small children: a boy, perhaps eight, who'd taken twenty rounds in a straight line from his groin to his jaw, and a six-year-old girl screaming at the top of her lungs, her legs stitched across by mini-gun fire. The soldier, a huge country grunt named Moose, cried, "We gotta check fire, man; they're all *kids* we're hitting!"

Smith turned the girl over, gaping at the huge exit wounds in her thighs. "Stay with the kid, we're gonna evac her," he yelled, and double-timed it across the hill to where his buddy Schoony was standing, looking down in a daze at another small girl. A 20-mm rocket had caught her square in the chest, peeling her open as bloodlessly as a can of new tennis balls. "We're killin' kids, man, do you fuckin' believe it?" croaked Schoony, too far gone to get his head down in a free-fire zone.

By now, the cry to *Check fire!* was general all over the hill. Stone cold line grunts threw their guns on the ground and carried the children to a little clearing, laying them down lovingly in a cordon of the dead. Others, disbelieving, kept screaming *Medic up!* but wherever the medics responded, there was nothing to be done. Nevertheless, they did everything, performing heroic medicine, clamping arterial gushers with one hand and tying off gunshot trauma with the other. There were twenty-five kids cut to pieces on that hill, and by the time the corpsmen had seen to the last of them, even their boots were soaked through with the ambient blood.

It fell to Smith and several others to bag up all the bodies; the rest of Delta Company was too done in by what they'd done. Some second lieutenant, a ninety-day wonder out of West Point, ran around the hill screaming, "Dig a hole, establish a perimeter!" but no one listened to him or stirred from where they'd sprawled, hacking up their horror in thick sobs and vomit. Even the captain, a lifer by the name of Murphy, was down on both knees with his head in his hands, crying his eyes out by the side of the LZ.

Working his way mechanically through the litter of corpses, Smith underwent a kind of reverse conversion, conceiving a huge hatred for his God and his country. A hot-burning kid who'd always lived his life like it was the last lap at Daytona, he suddenly felt everything go ice-cold dead in him, including his tears, which were flash frozen in their ducts. Zippering the children into preposterously big body bags and loading them into the back of a Chinook, he felt nothing but a numbing, arctic rage, and the more he looked into the faces of the dead, the frostier he became. From that day forth, nothing mattered anymore, nothing lived in his heart but the memory of those kids. That night, in the foxhole he shared with Schoony, he saw them afresh every time he closed his eyes, smelling the cordite and gunsmoke and copper-scented blood. Body rushes broke over him like the big waves at China Beach, doubling him up with nausea and beating his heart out of his chest. Mercilessly, he brought himself up on charges, ignoring the fact that he hadn't even had time to fire his weapon. No matter; there was no plea-bargaining his conscience. It found him guilty of mass murder by association, and sentenced him to life of psychic imprisonment, with little or no hope of appeal.

A couple of hours after the massacre, word got around the LZ that the slain children were woodcutters, sent up from the village below to gather twigs and branches for firewood. Instantly, Delta Company came out of its stupor and started digging deep trenches as fast as it could, certain that the fathers of those kids would overrun them come nightfall, backed by a couple of hundred VC for good measure. On the north corner of the hill, Smith and Schoony lined their hole out, and contrived a crude overhang of sandbags and logs. Sitting beneath it waiting for the daylight to fail, they listened to the bitter chatter from the other hootches, hearing the words *My Lai* again and again. Aroused, Smith dashed off a letter to Ted Kennedy, reporting in full detail what he'd witnessed that morning. He took care to name no names— he'd never rat out his brothers—but he had to tell *someone* what he'd just been through. Although choppers had buzzed in and out of the hill all day, bringing a suite of brass through to inspect the scene, no one had bothered to debrief the men, either to walk them through the fuckup or to meet them in their grief. That was the law of the jungle in 'Nam: shit happened, and no one said a second word about it. In this 24-hour-a-day war, no one had time for your tears or your battered heart. It has taken us twenty years—and tens of thousands of 'Nam vet suicides—to finally see that silence for what it is: a long fuse attached to a very big bomb.

Those three nights on the tattered hill near Da Nang, no one in Delta Company got two hours' sleep. Chain-smoking Marlboros and slurping mouthfuls of speed, they locked in on the treeline fifty yards below and opened up every time a breeze kissed a bough. If one man saw a ghost, then all of them saw it, unleashing wild fusillades that lasted several minutes. But in the morning, still wound as tight as ten-dollar watches, they searched the brush futilely for bodies or a blood trail. *Fuck you, Charlie, when the hell you gonna show?* they snarled, almost longing, by that last night, for a return of fire, for some definitive second act in this lunatic tragedy. It never came, however, and the next day, they found out why. According to the LT, who'd just gotten it over the radio from Battalion, some behind-the-scenes player from Army Intelligence had gone to the chief of the village shortly after the massacre and arrived at a deal with him. Bowing and scraping through his ARVN translator, he'd apologized profusely for the "unforeseeable error," and negotiated a cash payment to the affected families. The agreed-upon price per dead child, said Battalion, was in the vicinity of $600.

ALL THESE HARD AND FRAUGHT YEARS LATER, Smith sits at a table on the top floor of his huge shelter and says, "I still see those kids at night nonstop, and I still don't sleep worth a damn. Bad things happen to me as I'm drifting off. I'll hear a rifle shot as loud as if it was next to my ear, or hear it in a deep sleep and wake up in the middle of an ambush. Hearing the crack of an AK[-47] and the *thoomp* of a mortar. Smelling the smell of dead people and dead vegetation. Whenever that happens, I lay awake for a long time, scared like a bastard that I'm gonna die in my sleep."

He twitches, embarrassed by this last admission, and leans over to light a cigarette, his fifth in half an hour. Like a lot of 'Nam grunts, Smith smokes incessantly; to be in a room with any three of them is to be mired in their blue haze and memories. "Of course, when I *first* came home, I couldn't sleep at all," he continues, letting out a fat contrail of smoke. "I'd just go and go and go till I passed out for two days, collapse in my mother's backyard. I couldn't sleep in the house, so I'd take her $200 quilt and bed down on the grass outside. Lay there all night, watching the stars and smoking a joint, obsessing about those kids, and the brothers I'd left behind there. . . ."

He goes quiet for half a minute, staring wanly out the window, monitoring a flutter of ghosts. All around him in his handsome, oak-paneled office, with its magisterial view of the Boston skyline, are the pomps and appurtenances of Smith's work—his slew of national service awards from veterans' organizations; the Presidential Seal appointing him the 142nd Point of Light; and framed pictures of himself at the Republican convention, where he brought down the Astrodome with his powerhouse speech about the plight of homeless veterans in America. But the subject is slain children, who inhabit his every silence, and Smith is scarcely basking in his glory.

"There was this orphanage just outside the wire of the

Da Nang airport, run by nuns for Amerasian children. Most of 'em were toddlers, beautiful three-year-old boys and girls, and whenever we came back from the field, I used to bring 'em whatever I could scrounge—food, clothing, bandages, medicine, anything I could get my hands on from the medics. One night, I'm listening to the radio in Battalion Aid, and somebody gets on the net screaming that the VC have hit an orphanage, and the Rough Puffs [the South Vietnamese National Guard] are getting their ass kicked all over the yard. I run over to the evac in Da Nang, and find out that the Cong have slaughtered half those kids straight off, and put the other half in the hospital with claymore wounds. To see those kids laying there maimed and bleeding, with huge bumps all over 'em from shrapnel entries—I knew then and there, if I didn't already, that this war was pure, fucking evil. Human life had no meaning there, it was completely without value—and I was no better than any of 'em."

THE YIELD OF ALL WAR IS DEATH AND DYSFUNC-tion, whatever you wind up calling it. In World War I, the name for battle-induced illness was *shell shock*, based in part on the quaint notion that it was the sonic violence of high explosives that rendered soldiers psychotic. By World War II, the working theory about "combat fatigue," as it had come to be known, propounded that the ill essentially suffered from too much war, as if war were a thing to be quantified, like exposure to radon, or the sun. This is by no means to scant the suffering of that war's afflicted, who are still warehoused by the tens of thousands in VA wards, waiting out their days in a fog of sedatives and neuroleptics, and an asphyxiating, stone-gray silence.

But if we are vastly more enlightened after the war in Vietnam about this illness born of horror, it is precisely because that war was so awash in horror. Every unhealed grunt has a memory or two that recur like tics in conversation. On the beach in Venice with Roy, it was his recitation, every twenty minutes, of finding a GI tied to a rubber tree, his body parts scattered around it like a jigsaw puzzle. Nor could Black Scotty stop favoring me with the story of a water buffalo that had been gutted and used for cover by a team of VC snipers. "Soon as we touched down in the goddamn chopper, gooks came flyin' out the bottom a' that buffalo, pickin' us off like it wasn't no thing. Cost us five men to finally grease those bastards, but when we did, we cut their dicks off and fed 'em to the dogs. I mean, fuck it, it was the only right thing to do, don't you think?"

Enough has been written elsewhere about what spawned that war's savagery that I won't repeat it here. Suffice it to say that nothing in their eight weeks at Fort Ord or Parris Island prepared American troops for what they found when they got off the plane in Da Nang. The vast majority of them were schoolkids a couple of months removed from their senior prom (in World War II, the average age of a GI was 26; in Vietnam it was 19). As perfectly ignorant about Southeast Asia as the men who sent them there, they found themselves monkey-in-the-middle of a people's war so barbaric that babies were routinely used as trip plates for bombs, and disemboweled cadavers swung from village gateposts, hideously evoking Dante: *"Abandon hope, all ye who enter here. . . ."*

In the public imagination, the war in Vietnam was fought principally by two kinds of kids: the thick-necked white boys from the Corn Belt and cadet academies who'd been raised in the low church of anticommunism and who

were hellbent to fight the red menace before it came march-
ing up Main Street; and the bitter black sons of the urban
underclass, who served and died in disproportionate numbers, and fragged their C.O.'s in protest. Few of the several
hundred vets I've talked to, however, answer to either
description, least of all Smith. He grew up the only boy in a
loving family of women on a quiet block in Newport,
where it was the dream of his devout Catholic mother and
four sisters that he become a priest. To that end, he spent
most of his childhood and adolescence under the roof of
Saint Mary's Cathedral: an altar boy at age 5; the keeper of
the keys at 10; an after-school counselor of Catholic doc-
trine at 14. Such, however, was his subsequent revolt that
by 16 his chief distinctions were rolling the best joints at De
La Salle Academy and talking a succession of parochial
school girls out of their blue plaid skirts in the back of his
'60 Impala.

"I'd figured out by then that I wasn't gonna be much of
a priest, as gaga as I was about getting high and getting
head," Smith laughs. "But my beef with the Church didn't
start for real until I got shipped over to Vietnam. Saw with
my own two eyes what kind of bloodbath the Church was
giving its blessing to. Sending its stooges around to the
evacs to whisper over guys with sucking chest wounds,
and pin Saint Francis medals on the worst of 'em. I tell you
right now, if there *is* a Jesus Christ and he came through
that goddamn window, I'd have some killer questions for
him. Like, 'Where the fuck were *you* in '71, when all those
babies and young boys were gettin' shot to ribbons? What,
did you take the year off, go on sabbatical somewhere? And
if you couldn't make it, why didn't you send your buddy
Buddha, or Mohammed?' Instead, all we got were these fat,
stoned padres, telling us, 'God is kind, God is infinitely

merciful.' Excuse me, but I was *there*, pal, and God was nothing of the kind. What he *was*, was missing in action."

When clinicians calibrate the psychic damage of Vietnam, they often speak of the sufferer's "trinity of loss"—his buddies, his youth, and his absolute moral innocence. But missing from the list, says George Mendoza, the shelter's PTSD director, is the bitter, pandemic death of faith. "For most of these guys, God and country were the same thing, a communion they'd believed in since they were three years old. They come from a proud line of warrior Catholics and Christians—their old men were the heroes of World War II, and their *old men's* old men were the same thing in World War I. So when the call came down in '68 or '70, *of course* they were going to answer it; it was all mixed up with father-love and the Holy Father."

Smith's tie with his forebears was largely presumptive: his father had succumbed to his wounds in the Korean War, and his grandfather, who'd fought so bravely in the Battle of Ardennes, was dead of cancer before Smith was out of grade school. But he was certainly susceptible to their martial influence, bodying forth from gray snapshots on the dining room wall and rendered audible in the fierce devotions of his maternal grandmother.

"She never stopped talking about either one of them, or about my uncles, either, for that matter, who'd all gone off to war and fought like the eyes of their mothers depended on it," says Smith. "I used to sit there in church every Sunday and think about that, listening to all the mothers crying for their kids who'd died in 'Nam. I'd hear that, and all I could think about was going over there and getting vengeance for them. Where I'm from, you didn't have to be GI Joe to hate gooks. All you hadda be was eighteen and Irish-Catholic."

*   *   *

AND SO, WHEN HE CAME OF AGE IN FEBRUARY
of 1971, Smith enlisted in the Army and accepted assign-
ment to Vietnam, spurning an automatic exemption as the
only son in his family. After eight weeks of basic training
and eight more with heavy weapons, he landed in-country
in the middle of July, and was assigned to a light infantry
brigade in the heart of I Corps, where the action was as
fierce and breathless as the weather. Indeed, so depleted
was Delta Company when he caught up with it that only
two platoons remained of the four with which it began. In
the furious endgame of the war, the 65-man unit had been
jerked up and down the coast, taking massive casualties
that had made a shambles of its morale. As Smith was heartsick to learn, any delusions of an American victory in
Vietnam had long since departed on a flight out of Da
Nang. Where as recently as December of 1970 there had
been 300,000 troops in-country, now there were less than
70,000, and those that remained were essentially being used
as bait. For weeks on end, Smith and his unit were sent out
on ambush, drawing fire from NVA regulars who were then
pummeled by U.S. artillery. The gambit was brutally effective, as it had been throughout the war, at locating and
obliterating large numbers of the enemy, but it was only
marginally less destructive of American lives. Smith tells the
story of a search-and-destroy op gone haywire, in which a
strike was called in on a VC rifle team in Charlie Ridge.

"We were split up, two squads of us, maybe thirty yards
apart in the brush, when someone in the forward squad
dimes in the guns," says Smith. "Next thing I know, a bun-
dle of airburst shells starts blowing, detonating ten to
twenty feet in the air and hurling the killing shit right at us.
Two or three guys were cut to ribbons by the shrapnel; the

rest of us caught chunks of it but lived to tell the tale. I was about the luckiest, I only got it in the leg, a frag that took out a piece of my shin. Naturally, of course, none of us got a Purple Heart for it. One of my biggest beefs with the VA is their obsession with the 'weight of the paper.' If there's no piece of paper saying that I got hit by shrapnel, then, by God, I guess it never happened. If there's no piece of paper saying I lost a leg in combat, then obviously I have *two* legs—regardless of what I'm standing on. Pardon me, *but there was a fucking war in progress, gentlemen*; it wasn't a god-damn *audit* we were conducting out there. More than half the crap that went down in combat was never recorded—and, over and over, the VA's used that trick to deny benefits to these guys.

"I'll give you a better example—my teeth. Sometime that winter, we were humping rice paddies in Elephant Valley, slogging through cold mud in a wide-open field. Suddenly, a barrage of sniper fire comes down—*boom*, everybody freaks out and breaks for cover. Me, I go running like a bastard for this dike when I trip and fall face-first into a knee-deep paddy. The sixty-pound ruck on my back knocks the wind out of me, and I start swallowing this horrible, black, shit-infested water—if someone hadn't turned me over and popped my ruck, I'd've drowned to death in thirty seconds in it.

"A couple of guys pull me up by the head, gagging and sneezing this shit up, and almost immediately, my face starts to blow up like a beach ball. I start running a huge fever, which gets worse by the hour, and by the time they get me to the hospital, I was completely delirious. Two days later, when I finally come out of the clouds, my mouth is so swollen it's like there's a chipmunk in both cheeks. What they'd done was to go in and pull all the molars out so they could stick these drains in my gums, and run IV antibiotics in there to kill the massive jaw infection. A week later, I'm up and going again, but now I've got no teeth left to chew with, and over the next six months, they pull the rest of the middle and back ones, too; apparently, the antibiotics had rotted 'em right out of my head.

"Anyway, the doc who did most of the work says, 'No problem, kid; when you get home, just go to the VA and they'll give you a mouthful of crowns.' Beautiful, I said, and as soon as I get back, I race like a doofus to the VA in Providence. There, Dr. I-Yank-'Em tells me he'll *take out* the few teeth I got left and give me a set of false choppers to use. Say *what*, I go? What about those crowns I was promised? 'Tough eggs,' he said, 'we got no paper on you; there's no evidence that you lost the teeth in 'Nam.' Hey, doc, *what about the evidence in front of your fuckin' eyes?* I'm a twenty-year-old kid in chinos and Bass Weejuns who never had a cavity in my life—where the hell *else* do you think I lost a mouthful of teeth?"

Smith bolts up to pour himself a cup of coffee, glowering as he slops in a full inch of milk. Cigarettes excepted, coffee seems to comprise his entire diet, which may explain, at least in part, why he is as gaunt and wired as he was in Quang Tri. At 42, his face is still improbably boyish, his front teeth complicating a corrosive grin, his pale skin taut over otherwise empty jaws. A tuna sandwich sits undisturbed by him, a bowl of ice cream melting beside it. "I eat, but it's a helluva lot of work, believe me. I just hope that somewhere down the line, I find me a 'Nam vet dentist, 'cause the last guy I went to quoted me twenty grand to do the work. I said, 'Yeah, sure, doc—do you take Vietnamese piasters?' I think I've still got a footlocker full of 'em in my mother's basement somewhere."

*   *   *

ONE OF THE FIRST THINGS YOU NOTICE ABOUT
the men in this shelter is how ineffably lonely they are. To
be sure, there are friendships made and refined, particularly
among the dozens of 'Nam combat vets, who hang out
together in their third-floor clubhouse adjoining George
Mendoza's office. But you quickly get the sense that those
bonds are provisional, a function of being in the same place
at the same time. None of the brothers seem to get too tight
for too long, lest one of them turn up dead someday with a
needle in his arm, or catch a hissy and go hide out in the
Everglades for a year. Most of the men shrug and acknowledge that it's been like this since the 'Nam, when a best
buddy died and broke their heart forever. After that, it just
seemed smarter to keep to themselves, and not put their
feelings out there to be trampled on again.

"I had a real good buddy in Da Nang," says Smith, "a
brother by the name of Chris that I used to smoke a bone
with and work the black market together. But after he got
waxed in a rocket attack, I didn't have another male friend
for fifteen years. That was the first thing I discovered when
I met Mark [Helberg, a co-founder of the shelter] and the
others in the combat support group—to be a 'Nam combat
vet, I don't care how many years later, was to feel like you
were the last fucking man on the planet."

It cannot have diminished that lunar aloneness that
every American who fought in Vietnam entered and left it
entirely on his own. In a war of attrition and twelve-month
hitches, you landed in-country not with your tight crew
from boot camp, nor certainly, God knows, with your old
pals from the buddy program, but as the single-file replace-
ment for a dead soldier somewhere. And when, a year to the
minute later, your tour was over, that chopper came for you

and nobody else, no matter what kind of nightmare your unit was pinned down under. Stories of wild and freaky departures are as common as grunt tattoos at the shelter, but I haven't heard many that top the one Smith tells.

"It was at the end of the most intense five days of the war for me, I mean nonstop madness from Da Nang to the Dong Ha River," says Smith. "This was around Easter of '72, and the NVA were just pouring down the Zee, whole entire *battalions* comin' across the bridge. They'd airlifted us north to Quang Tri to meet 'em, and no sooner do we hit the tarmac than we're in a world of pain. Charlie'd taken the airport from the ARVN marines, and for three days and three nights, we went building to building with 'em, working our way to the tower in one monster firefight. Meanwhile, out there in the hills somewhere, they must've captured a couple of ARVN pieces, because Charlie laid down some killer incoming on us—I'm talking five-fives and *seven*-fives, the Queen Mother of battle. We lost a shitload of guys underneath that fire, and for the first time in my tour, I started to know how Charlie felt, sitting there all night waitin' for the hammer to drop. After three nights of that, no letup, plus all the shit *we* were droppin' on him—just wave after wave of Skyhawks and Phantoms—I didn't think *any* of us was gonna get up and walk away. Figured they'd just bury us all there, twenty yards from each other, and roll it all over with like a fresh strip of tarmac.

"But by day four, we had dropped so much murder on his position that we actually had a hard time recovering the bodies. I mean, yeah, we found like a couple of dozen in the rubble, but it was spooky, like Khe Sanh—where the hell did the rest of 'em go? Even in death, you know, Charlie liked to fuck with your head, which might've been one of the reasons there was so much mutilation going on—guys figured if they could just cut 'em up into enough pieces, maybe they wouldn't come after you again.

"Anyway, when we got our shit together and figured out who was still breathing, they threw us in with some bastard elements of the Americal, going north to the Dong Ha River. We were in this convoy of tracks and deuce-and-a-halfs, and streaming down the road past us, going south to Da Nang, were I-don't-know-how-many thousands of refugees fleeing the enemy. A lot of 'em were ARVNs, whole companies of 'em at a shot, knocking women and children down in their hurry to *di-di-mao*. We're screaming, 'Hey, motherfuckers, this is *your* war we're fighting; why'n't ya stick around a while, find out how it all turns out?' But they're like, 'So sorry, GI, no time to fight. Got to get to New York, open all-night grocery.'

"Suddenly, out of nowhere, comes this gigantic clap of thunder, and a hot wind whooshing by with, like, shrapnel and body parts. I look up—somehow, I'm flat on my back in the road, and up ahead maybe fifty yards there's three tracks of ours burning, pouring out flames through the TC hatch. Instinctively, I run forward, going to the one on the right, and it's got a huge hole in the center of it and the back door's down, and a kid's lying in the doorway, just crushed like a pancake. As I reach for him, another round comes in, just behind and to the left of me. Now there's smoke and gas fire and the smell of burnt flesh everywhere, and I run to the middle track and pull two guys out, both of 'em burning up like I can't even describe to you.

"By now, other guys have come running forward, and they're throwing dirt as fast as they can on the middle track, trying to put the fire out, but it's useless, forget about it, the thing is just completely engulfed in flames, and inside we can hear the *pow-pow-pow* of ammo cooking off. Up ahead now, another huge round comes in, our own one-seven-five shells bustin' our ass, and there's complete fucking chaos and mass hysteria, and I run left to the third track—it's laying in a low culvert—and a guy comes crawling out of it with his whole face bloody, I mean a scalp lac from hell that is just pouring down blood. He's screaming out somebody's name and fighting me off to go back in for him and I look inside and see the driver and there's nothing left of his chest. I just stood there, stone frozen, I couldn't get either of my legs to work, and another guy yells, 'Move out, man, there's gas everywhere in there!' The last thing I remember, I'm on my knees in the road hypnotized, wondering how something made of six-inch steel could just burn up like a pile a' rags."

When the barrage gave out, wheeling a klick or so up the road, Smith fell in with the other grunts in his company for two hours of horror duty—bagging and tagging the remains of thirty grunts. As they worked, several of the men fell down in a dead faint, overcome by the heat and the unimaginable stench, but Smith, as he invariably did in these matters, slid deep into a fierce, robotic trance, steeping himself in a tantric sense of betrayal as he worked.

"I kept saying to myself over and over, 'Those are *our* guns that did this, we *made* those damn shells; my country is killing my brothers.' Something happened to me right there, I don't know how to explain it, but it was like suddenly I got what the whole war was about. It wasn't about communism or preserving democracy or any of that other happy shit; it wasn't even really about staying alive. It was about dropping all these bombs so General Dynamics could make its nut off us, and it didn't even matter who all they landed on. Us, them—what the fuck was the difference? Just ship 'em, drop 'em, and make some more. If they fall on our own kids, fuck it; send their mom a gold star. She can always put it on top of her little tree for Christmas."

Forty-eight hours later, still in the clutches of that calcine rage, Smith was digging a trench above the Dong Ha River when a Huey swooped in. "Get on it, you're outta here," said his bluff LT. "Go home and hump your girlfriend once for the rest of us."

Smith stood there in stop-time, the blood whooshing around his ears, speechless for the first and last time in his life.

"G'bye, Smith, see ya. And leave your pack and rifle here. You don't even have time for a piss farewell."

Smith stumbled onto the bird, caught another one in Quang Tri, and within an hour was boarding a 747 in Da Nang. In one of those eldritch touches that speaks volumes about the Army, a staff sergeant handed him a first-class ticket on Pan Am, and sent him aboard, unbathed, in the gore-spattered fatigues he'd been wearing for six days. No sooner had he taken his seat up front than the whole section bellied out, all the brass and corporate spooks diving rear-ward, holding their noses. "Yeah, well, that's what the war smells like, you REMF bastards!" Smith yelled after them, and ordered up the first in a series of Johnny-on-the-rocks. By the time he touched down in Oakland, he was more bombed than the Hai Van Pass, and his eyes were swollen shut from fat blunts of opiated dope.

"I just sat there, determined to get blown out of my mind—and the more I got wasted, the worse it all came back on me: the stink of burnt grunt shit and J-4 jet fuel; the sight of that kid in the track with his whole chest gone. It was a twenty-two-hour plane ride, and I'm flashing all the way home, livin' those eight months out in like a slo-mo seizure. People think of flashbacks as this wild and violent freak-out, but for me it's like being strapped down and watching *Platoon* from the front row. It goes on and on and loops back and there isn't a damn thing you can do about it, all the shit you did and didn't do over there bombarding you like a bastard. *This*, you see, is what happens when you don't debrief your troops, when you shut 'em down, red-hot from combat, and stick 'em on a plane. In Israel, when they pull a kid from the field, they give him as much support and counseling as he needs. Is that expensive to do? Probably, but did you ever see a homeless vet in Jerusalem? Whereas here, where the VA doesn't give a fuck for its kids, the shelters are packed solid with 'Nam and Desert Storm heroes. You tell *me* which is the more expensive approach."

IT SAYS EVERYTHING ABOUT THE THOROUGHGO-ing shamefulness of that war that Ken Smith and the other combat vets in his shelter came back from it not as honored sons and soldiers, but like skulking hoods in a witness protection program. To be sure, you don't throw a Times Square parade for the troops of a botched and hateful conflict, but it is almost as if there was some tacit arrangement at the top to make the homecoming of Vietnam veterans as ignoble as possible. Typically, their plane landed at three in the morning, where, under cover of darkness, they were hustled onto waiting buses and spirited out the back gate to Travis Air Force Base in Oakland. Inexplicably, however, just thirty-six hours later, they were ordered to reboard those buses in their conspicuous dress A's, and driven straight into the teeth of a howling mob, who merrily pelted them with raw eggs and pigs' blood.

"It was amazing, it was exactly like being back in the 'Nam," recalls Warren Quinlan, the shelter's former director of operations. "You were in this crazy place, everyone there wanted to kill you, and to help 'em do it, the Army'd dressed you up in a big, green bull's-eye. I mean, fuck it, man, if you're too ashamed of us to hire a band, then at least lay down some cover so we can get out the back door. Spare us the pain, at least for another forty-eight hours, of seeing how much our own people hate our guts, of how mothers are gonna be draggin' their little kids indoors whenever they see us coming."

For many of the men I've talked to, that hazing in Oakland (and the one that inevitably followed it in their hometown airport) was the straw that broke their back. A number of them, like shelter co-founder Mark Helberg, went deep into hiding for years and years, living alone in an attic or wild in the woods and coming out only when they ran out of beer or dope. Others "went over the mountain," as they say in 'Nam-vetspeak, settling like Kurtz in the jungles of Laos or Thailand, never to be heard from again. And countless thousands more ran back to their buddies in-country, unable to tread the path of mute humiliation here.

"I shouldn'ta never come home from the 'Nam—home didn't exist for me no more," said Jimmy Nalls, a vet on the beach in Venice who was so perfectly pasted with grime that it was impossible to tell where it ended and his beard began. "I'd rather a' been up on that black wall [in Washington] than here in this black hole—and I'm sure my old man and lady wishes I was, too."

"Everyone in this shelter has a horror story [about coming home]—some days, that's all they want to talk to me about," says Mendoza, the PTSD director. "They're so angry about it still, and so hurt and heartbroken, that it just eats them up like cancer. They keep saying to me, 'I don't understand it, George, I made this sacrifice because I loved my country, and when I came home, my country hated me for it.' They're sitting there in their living room with all this torment inside them, and even their own mother's acting like the whole thing never happened. That's why so many of them thought they were going crazy, and then the flashbacks started, and the nightmares, and then they *really* thought they were nuts. One of the great moments in group is when they find out they *all* thought that, that *all* of them hid in the basement so no one could hear them crying their eyes out. That's a huge discovery for these guys, not only because they see they weren't crazy after all, but also that they weren't the only ones singled out for this kind of abuse. There's forty or fifty guys in here that went through the exact same thing they did."

One of them is Smith, who still seethes over his return. He tells the story freely, drawing fresh juice off its circuit, but there is something in the recitation besides hurt and rage, a kind of bafflement that begs to be put straight after all these years. He'd done everything by the book, he says, the day that he came home, ditching anything that smacked of Army on him—throwing his medals and dress greens into the garbage in San Francisco, and tricking himself out in hideous thrift-shop rags. He'd even picked up a suitcase so he wouldn't be seen lugging around a duffel bag, and when he landed at Logan Airport in Boston that afternoon, he calmly strolled through the terminal, clearing the by-now inevitable cordon of protesters.

But downstairs in the baggage room, waiting by the carousel for his luggage, he came under the cool scrutiny of three teenage girls, two of whom held up picket signs. The third, spotting Smith's lone oversight—the shit-encrusted combat boots underneath his sweat pants—went up to him and shouted, "You! You're in the U.S. military, aren't you! You just came back from killing babies, didn't you!"

About what happened next, Smith isn't especially proud, but neither is he apologetic. In his defense, he says merely that the Ken Smith raised by a mother and four sisters was instructed never to strike a woman; *that* Ken Smith, however, he adds, never came back from 'Nam. "I turned around and this face was literally three inches from mine, glaring at me with the most fierce fuckin' hatred. *Click,* I lost it right there, and in one clean motion, dropped my suitcase and drilled her square in the middle of her fucking forehead. She hits the floor out cold, and I mean bleeding like a pig, and now I'm after the other two but they screwed out in a hurry, and I'm standin' there just *gone,* man, in my own little mad minute. I don't know what you'd call it, it was nothing like a flashback; I was right there but *flooded,* you know? Just stoned on fucking rage.

"See, there's an igniter in every Vietnam combat vet, a switch that gets thrown and then he goes to general quarters on you. For me, it's hearing some know-nothing asshole disrespect the honor and efforts of my brothers. We went over there and you didn't, and we lost too much doing it, so if you want to talk about 'Nam, confine yourself to talking about the war. You haven't even *begun* to earn the right to talk about the warriors."

In any case, the girl he hit was only too happy to prefer charges, and Smith spent several hours in the airport lockup waiting to be arraigned. Though he was still profoundly stoned and essentially unslept for seven days, two thoughts presented themselves to him front and center: one, that for all his eight months and five days of spotless service in 'Nam, he would undoubtedly be drummed out of the Army for this; and, two, he was good and goddamned dangerous around the general public. Whatever else happened, he had to get the hell away from people; maybe gather up his tent and go hide out in the Rockies for a while. Let the deer and the antelope talk him down from some of this.

Just before the cops came to haul him off, a state trooper peered into Smith's cell. "You Army?" he scowled. "Just back from the 'Nam?"

Smith nodded; the trooper disappeared for a couple of minutes, then came back jangling a fat ring of keys. Parading Smith in handcuffs through the terminal at rush hour, he deposited him in the back of a blue-black cruiser and drove for better than an hour in brick-oven silence. When he came to the state line, he handed him over to a Rhode Island trooper, who drove him the rest of the way home to Newport. Depositing Smith and his suitcase on the steps of his mother's front porch, the trooper uncuffed him and put a hand on his shoulder.

"I don't know, kid, I wasn't over there, and maybe it was as fucked-up as everyone tells you," he said. "But if you're smart, you'll make like none of it ever happened. Just go back to loving your country, it's the only one you got—and stay the hell away from Boston, you hear me?"

No one answered when Smith knocked on the door of his house (he'd been too spaced to phone ahead from the airport in San Francisco), and so he broke in through a downstairs window, dropped his luggage in the hallway, and went out for what turned into a ten-hour walk. "I must've gone the radius of Newport two times, freaking out and crying and wondering where the hell I was gonna go," he says. "I was sick in the head and hurtin' like a bastard and needed someplace safe to lay down for a while, but I knew it wasn't gonna be *there*, that much was obvious from the airport. In fact, as I'm walking along the road there, I'm constantly checking out the area around me, scanning my back and perimeter for *someone*, I can just *feel* him out there watching. My mind is going twice the speed of sound, every sense is kicking in, information meltdown, and all I keep thinking about is that girl in the terminal, those eyes just screamin' at me like VC tracers. Before that, believe me, I was plenty fuckin' evil, so much hate inside me that I had to run away from my family and not be heard from for ten years.

"But even with all that, there was some piece still of *me* in there, the kid who loved his family, and dreamed of 460 Mustangs, and told Jesus jokes whenever there was a stray Catholic in the room. *That* kid died the day I landed at Logan. *Eight fucking months I'm on my hands and knees over there, pulling dead kids out of bombed-out tanks, each of 'em burnt so bad their damn skin came off in your hands—and for what? Where's the big payoff for Specialist Ken Smith? To have some little Back Bay cunt spit all over me and scream murder like I just killed her lap dog, Toto? To come home from killing VC and find out that now I'M the VC, I'M the gook that everyone wants to kill over here? Well, thanks but no thanks, and fuck you with a broomstick, my fellow Americans; that's one betrayal I'll never forgive you for. I mean, yeah, I love my country and I hate my enemies—but sometimes I have a little problem tellin' the two apart.*"

"RAGE? IT'S THE COIN OF THE REALM AROUND here; it's what they use instead of gas or oil to heat this place," says Leslie Lightfoot, the tall, lovely, Ann Taylor–elegant therapist who does a lot of the one-on-one trauma work at the shelter. Your first thought upon meeting her is, How the hell does *she* survive here? But two minutes into idle conversation with her, you see she's about as soft as the barrel of an M-60. "That's one reason the VA's been so ineffective with these men—it's scared to death of them. They come in off the street with a huge chip on their shoulder, and the first thing the triage nurse thinks is, Drug 'em, drug 'em!—which is exactly how to *not* treat their anger. It just keeps it in amber, keeps it buried for another year, when what it really needs to heal is *air*, and lots of it. Get it said, get it out of you, let someone who cares about you hear it. That, in one word, is why this works and the VA doesn't— we *care* about these guys, they mean everything to us, because at some level or other, they *are* us. You can't do this work strictly from the standpoint of book-stuff—either you're a vet like they are and have been through some hell of your own, or as a rule, they won't engage with you."

Lightfoot, 44, was a 'Nam-era medic stationed in a hospital in Germany for two years. Though she had no firsthand experience of combat trauma, she certainly saw enough of it in the eyes of the men routed through there to be bitterly and permanently moved by it. "Even the ones who weren't wounded, like the medics with time left, were in such pain that they immediately got strung out on heroin, which was cheap and all over the place back then in Lannstuhl. I'm still haunted by one guy, this beautiful kid in my ward, who made me a silver peace sign before he left. As dumb and nineteen as I was at the time, I'd no idea what he meant by that. It took me ten, fifteen years, and a lot of rear-view guilt, to figure out how desperately he needed to unload.

"But getting back to rage, one of the things you learn about it fast is how many different things it means. Sure, a lot of the time, it means exactly what it says it means: I hate you, Sergeant So-and-So, for making me torch that ville; I hate you, U.S. Marine Corps, for making me see what no human being was ever supposed to see. But a lot of the time, it's about the uncried tears of that twenty-year-old kid, who buried all those buddies at Hue or Con Thien and never got a chance to grieve them. If you can sit here and listen to it, I mean *really* listen to it, without flinching or gagging or backing away from it, you can get in there and help them feel what's been underneath it for all these years."

And what's it like to be alone in a room with a vet in the grip of that rage?

"Well, you can't be afraid of anger and do anger work," she says flatly. "But let's be very clear about something—it isn't PTSD that triggers a guy's violence; it's the booze and the drugs he's dosing himself with. I've been doing this work now for fourteen years, treating some of the angriest men on the planet, and only once have I felt my safety in peril from them. On the other hand, I *lived* with a 'Nam vet who got strung out on drugs, and *he* beat the living hell out of me. The bottom line is, as long as these guys have the heart to show up sober—and, believe me, that's the *only* way they're getting past those guards out there—I'll take my chances behind a closed door with them."

There is a knock on the door. Her eleven o'clock is here, a man with the pallor of an underwater corpse, and beautiful, doom-cast eyes.

"I mean, look, it would be ridiculous of me to say there was zero risk involved," she says, showing me out. "But I cherish these men; they're nothing less than heroes to me. And if I learned anything at all from three years in the service, it's that you don't go back for your wounded without taking some sort of risk."

*   *   *

ABOUT KEN SMITH'S RAGE, AT ANY RATE, LITTLE more need be said. It is bottomless, indiscriminate, the water in which he swims. Out of it grows this towering, generous thing, which has saved the lives of thousands and will save countless thousands more. But twenty years ago, there was nothing but poison in his rage, a kind of fast-twitch mayhem that nearly finished him off, and bullied his dumbstruck family. Four nights out of five, his first year back, he'd stagger home shit-faced from the shoreline bars, his face as bruised and mottled as a heel of skinned sausage. It wasn't enough for Smith to get thrashed by the biggest tough he could find, or have his head handed to him by the stove-bellied bouncers; no, *he* had to take on half the joint, calling out the mobs of sailors just back from the South China Sea as "a bunch of pussies and liars."

"I'd go up to 'em and yell, 'Quit tellin' war stories, ya bastards; what fuckin' war were *you* ever in? The only sailors *I* saw in 'Nam were twenty miles out to sea, eatin' pot roast and mashed potatoes and sleepin' in warm beds with clean sheets on 'em.' They'd look at me like maybe I'd caught a mortar or two in the head, and just before they jumped me, they'd ask what service *I* was in. 'The *Army*,' I'd go, 'the service that *fights*, but, you know, we actually appreciated you girls in the Navy. You gave us a ride whenever we needed to go somewhere and kill us a bunch of gooks.'

Those fights, it scarcely needs to be said, didn't go on for very long. Smith, all of 140 pounds when he came home from the jungle, would unleash his three or four wild shots, then get knocked around the room like a captured VC. But that, he says, was precisely the point—"to hurt and to *be* hurt, to have someone beat the war clean out of me. Sure, it would've been easier going to therapy, I guess, but that wasn't exactly part of the local technology where I'm from. I mean, I'd tell my mother how bad I was hurtin' and that I needed to get some help, and she'd bake me these big trays of chocolate chip cookies. Mom, I love you to death and I'm sorry for all the pain I know I caused you, but if chocolate chip cookies cured PTSD, I'd be the Joyce fuckin' Brothers of Keebler elves.

"That was the worst part of all, worse than being sick even and thinking no one could help me—looking into my mother's face and seeing how much pain *she* was in, watching her only son bleed from an internal gusher and being totally unable to help me. I know now, of course, that there are hundreds of thousands of women just like her out there, mothers and wives who are totally helpless and clueless, and rightfully scared out of their minds. That's why hundreds of thousands of us ran away from them in the first place—we were scared shit we'd kill them, or beat 'em beyond recognition. I know I, at least, came within an inch of murdering my sisters—and they hadn't done a damn thing to trigger it, either."

If there are tears left in Smith, they are largely untapped; he has wept only once, he says, in the last twenty years—his first trip to the Wall back in 1987, when he "spilt the whole load of 'em in a five-hour jag, and almost drowned on dry land doing it." But he gets detectably moist when he talks about his family, and the hell he put them through for ten or twelve years.

"All they wanted to do was love me back to the old Ken Smith, especially the youngest one, Joanie, who absolutely adored me. Instead, I tore the house up, and threw the table over at Thanksgiving dinner, and booby-trapped my bedroom with a homemade claymore—a couple of shotgun shells strung to a wire and hammer. I couldn't help it, I just *knew* the VC were out there somewhere, and was determined to get them before they came and got me. I was drunk or stoned constantly, going through an ounce of herb a week, the most mind-fucking Thai smoke that I'd sent home from the war by the footlocker. I couldn't eat, I barely slept, I'd just sit there alone in my bunker, smoking and thinking myself into a panic. And when it got so bad for me that the walls started moving, I'd up and disappear for a month. Just get on a plane and go hide out in Chicago, or Toronto. Let my mother think I was laying dead in some alley somewhere.

"But the thing that made me cut out for good, finally—and that still wakes me up screaming sometimes at four in the morning—is what I almost did to my little sister Joanie one night. I had come rolling in from the bars about two in the morning, and was sitting there in the living room smoking cigarettes and brooding about 'Nam. Sometime around dawn, I guess, I must've fallen out, because Joanie, who was all of twelve at the time and just the absolute peach of the planet, came down and found me passed out with a lit cigarette between my fingers. *Verrry* gently, she tried to take the butt out of my hand—and the next thing she knows, I've got her by the hair on the floor, and I'm about to smash her nose through her brain with my elbow. I had the elbow cocked and had begun to bring it down when I came to and caught myself in the middle of the stroke and——"

He breaks off, his breath going fast and shallow. *"Man, the look in her eyes then, the fucking terror I saw there, so much fear she couldn't even move her mouth to scream—"*

He stops again and looks away, his face ruddy with old self-hatred. "That was it, man. End of subject. I was unfit for human consumption. I got out of there and stayed out till I could trust myself in a room with 'em. Ten years away, living like an animal under a rock—no phone calls, no letters home saying, 'Hi, Mom, I'm alive and I hope you are, too. . . .'"

Another pause, another stricken stare out the window, transfixed by the pictures of his bitter inner life. Through a chink in his eyes, you suddenly see what Lightfoot was talking about—the vast recesses of guilt and sadness behind the sclera of rage. Some men in his care live immersed in it, are so steeped in anguish and desperate for unction that they give it all up to you directly, confessing to crimes of the most exquisite cruelty five minutes after making your acquaintance. Not so Smith, who is as well defended as Fort Knox. You get a glimpse of this sort of passage in him maybe once a decade.

"You told me you'd managed to forgive yourself, finally, for what you did in Vietnam," I say. "You think you'll ever forgive yourself for what you did back here?"

Smith lights a cigarette and takes a long pull on it, his damp eyes glowing in the late winter dusk. "I don't know how this is gonna come out and I don't really care, but I'm actually *grateful* I went to Vietnam. It stood me on my ear, made me someone worth being, instead of the punk who went over there thinking the world was his servant. And above and beyond that, it gave me this mission, to go back and take care of my wounded brothers.

"But what I keep thinking about is, what did *my mother* do to deserve this? It wasn't *her* war, *she* didn't go over there; she didn't torch villes or cut the ears offa gooks. What the fuck did *she* ever do to bring on what I did to her? *That's* the thing I can't seem to work out, y'know?"

A DOZEN YEARS BLEW BY IN A WHITE PHOSPHO-rous blur. Smith left home in the spring of 1974 and threw in with some hard-nut grunts from 'Nam, making a pile of money on speed-freak gambits—sailing tons of dope from Cartagena to Ocho Rios; smuggling the families of IRA fugitives into the States and resettling them down south. When that busted up after a year or two, there followed a maniacal stint at a large chain of steak joints, where, as manager, Smith tyrannized his wait-staff of college students, their punishment, no doubt, for having 'scaped hanging in 'Nam.

As clinicians like Lightfoot tell you, there are vets whose drug of choice is neither alcohol nor cocaine. It is, instead, a seventy-hour work week, and for years, Smith went at it like a windup madman, working twelve-hour days till he fell down from exhaustion and slept dreamlessly for two days straight. He worked Christmas Eves and Memorial Days, obliterating every spare second, driven, at least cognitively, by the straw goal of corporate advancement. Indeed, the day the company rewarded him with a regional vice presidency, Smith stalked off as if he'd just been royally insulted, and never set foot in one of their restaurants again.

"It blew their fucking minds—they'd never offered that kind of dough to a twenty-seven-year-old kid before—but then again, they'd never dealt with a fried 'Nam vet before, either," says Smith. "I was so full of poison and hatred of myself that success was like a shovel in the back in the head—I didn't know what the hell'd hit me there. Years later, I come to find out that that's happened to a lot of 'Nam grunts, getting totally demolished by a little success. When you're carrying around so much guilt that it's a fuckin' coin flip every day whether you even deserve to be *alive*, it's real screwy to hear someone tell you you rate a pay raise and a promotion.

"In fact, after about the fifth guy in this place that we won a nice, fat pension for—and thirty grand in back pay from the VA—took his check and drank himself to hell with it, we established a new set of guidelines here. Number one, the VA pays the money to us; we pay it out to you in weekly installments. Number two, if you decide to wander off for a month, or miss a bunch of meetings with your substance abuse counselor, we take that thirty grand and send it back to the VA—and good luck getting it out of them again without our legal assistance. As I tell these guys over and over again at the Monday night town meetings, I'm not in the co-dependent business. You snooze, you lose, and end of fucking subject. Go find some other sucker to carry your rucksack. I got my own freight to bear."

Having spurned, in any case, the job he put in seven years of Sundays to get, Smith went into the line of work that had been waiting in trust for him since 'Nam—manning an ambulance as an EMS cowboy in Boston. Within a week of pulling his first shift behind a stretcher, Smith was powerfully and progressively addicted; the speed rush was as wicked as it had been in the jungle.

"Man, the energy of being first on the scene of an accident, cutting some kid out of a pileup or screaming off with a serious burn victim—*that's* what I'd been missing since the day I left the 'Nam," says Smith. "You know, everyone talks about the weed and opium there, but for me the biggest drug was pure adrenaline. That fear and the wildness of being in a big-time firefight, the blood going through you with all that death firing around—I'll tell you what, man, if that didn't drive you crazy, pretty soon you found yourself starting to crave it. And when you got it, everything that was wrong with your little dogshit life—the boredom, the short money, the no women and no friends—all that crap went right out the window, and you were high like you've never been before or since.

"That, by the way, is why so many grunts became cops

and firemen here; we needed that fuckin' jolt, boy, that heart-in-the-throat blood rush. There's two kinds of junkies that came back from 'Nam—the kind that did drugs to try and forget it, and the kind that did drugs to try and relive it. For me, the drug of choice was that dispatch radio, and whenever a call came over it, I was amped like a bastard— *get some, get some, get some, motherfucker.*"

Get some, of course, was the battle cry of 'Nam, a grunt's injunction to his bullets or his mortar: *Go out and get me some gook KIAs.* But Smith's utterance of it in this context makes a certain condign sense. His shelter is full of men who have spent a significant portion of their lives in unconscious re-creations of the war, trying in their purblind way to make it come out right this time, and get some absolution in the bargain. There is Cuzzy Randall, an overinvolved line medic in the Army, who lost one kid after another under the triple canopy of Pleiku and who put in a dozen years back home working with troubled children before it kayoed him with degenerative colitis. There is John Nolen, Smith's boot-tough chief of security, who as a young MP, atop the U.S. Embassy, shoved Vietnamese women off transport choppers in the last evil hours before the fall of Saigon and spent the next ten years trying to make it up to the mothers of Roxbury as a devoted vice cop.

"Part of the pathology of trauma is the compulsion to play it out again, to get stuck inside the loop of the event that damaged you," Dr. Jonathan Shay, the psychiatrist at the VA, told me. "That would explain, by the way, why you found so many vets on the beach in Venice. The palm trees and the climate there, all that sixties psychedelia—physically, it's a dead ringer for Vietnam to those guys, and has a strong, affective hold on them. The fact is, they never *did* come home from the war, and are still bogged down in-country somewhere, looking for a way out. I can't imagine too many of them are going to find it on the beach, though. No matter how bad the conditions are there—and I'm sure they're quite awful—there *is* a certain comfort in sameness."

A LOT OF VIETNAM VETS ARE DECEPTIVELY EASY to spot: they "wear the 'Nam jacket," as the clinicians say, putting the war and its trappings out there like a gun-fighter's challenge, daring you to go for yours. But check the discharge papers on all those guys telling war stories, and you'll find that a third of them never got within twenty klicks of a firefight, and another third did their entire tour in Dusseldorf or Fort Dix. Indeed, the lying about that war has become so prevalent that therapists like Lightfoot now view it as a distinct pathology and accept no one's word about his service in Vietnam without seeing his discharge papers. "The [DD]214 form isn't a perfect document, but at least it will tell you whether he was in-country or not," says Lightfoot. "And if it shows a CIB [Combat Infantry Badge], then you pretty well know he saw action. How much and what kind is still anybody's guess, but I can tell you this much with total confidence—if you run into a guy who likes to *talk* about that war, bet the house and the car he didn't fight it."

The inverse, she goes on to add, is just as often true: that many of the men who *did* fight the war are impossible to spot, no matter how practiced your eye. They dress like tax attorneys or copier salesmen, talk endlessly about their jobs or their twelve-stroke handicaps, and disavow the war even if asked about it directly. But beneath that chirpy calm, she says, they are paddling for their lives, wild and terrified of the dark thing lurking below. Some of them are honorable husbands and fathers, shielding their loved ones from the sickness in their souls; others are monsters of random cruelty, ruling by the edict of their hair-trigger moods. But all of them have one thing of consequence in common: they are deeply, desperately, miserably alone, and incapable of imagining themselves otherwise. They have no combat buddies, unlike the guys in the "'Nam jacket," whom they see down in front at Veterans' Day parades, lying to one another about taking out mortars with grenade tosses and killing NVA regulars in hand-to-hand combat. (Sneered one vet at the shelter, with a chestful of ribbons as his witness, "If Charlie ever got within *five meters* of you, you were guaranteed going home in a silver box.") From the bunker of his avoidance, the covert vet thinks that *all* 'Nam vets are like that, that he alone is trapped inside his hyperbaric silence. It is killing him to keep his mouth shut, and at some level or other, he knows that, but to whom, after all these years of lock-down, is he supposed to go and spill his heart now?

"I tell you, I was really losing it, man, it was all startin' to come crumbling down on me, and there was no one—and I mean *no one*—for me to go and talk to," says Smith of his darkest period, the middle eighties. "I was flashin' all over the place, havin' nightmares that were tearin' my heart out, and when I was awake, which was pretty much around the clock, I was scared shit that I was having a [sanity] meltdown. To take my mind off it, I was working just insane hours, eighteen-, twenty-four-, thirty-six-hour shifts, catchin' two-hour naps in the back of the ambulance, and gulping speed like Saint Joseph's aspirin. The pressure in my head was like a fuckin' arc-light raid, and I felt like any minute now, something's gonna snap off inside me, but I'm fightin' it, man, runnin' *hard*, you know? Beggin' everybody and his brother for shifts. I didn't even want the money, I had no time to spend it, anyway. Just please don't make me go home to my empty apartment and lay there awake all night.

"And then one day, I'm walking somewhere, it's maybe eight o'clock in the morning, and I can barely move my feet after I-don't-know-how-many straight shifts now. I'm walkin' down Storrow Drive there, the Boston side of the Charles River, when all of a sudden, this chopper swoops by right over my head, making for Mass General [Hospital]. *Ba-BOOM!* It fuckin' hits me, the mother of all flashbacks, and I'm down on my knees with my hands over my ears, but it's *deafening*, man, the incoming, it's just pounding and pounding. I hear little kids screaming and mike-mikes firin' out, and smell the smell of all those burnt grunts inside the TC hatch, and I'm gaggin' and pukin' up all over the place, pukin' like I never once did in 'Nam. It goes on and on for what feels like hours to me, and now people are comin' over and going, 'Are you all right, should we call an ambulance?' and I'm like, 'Get away from me! Leave me the fuck alone!' and they screwed out and I'm just layin' there, soaked in sweat. A beautiful fall day, with a stiff breeze coming in from the river, and all I remember is sweatin' like I'm back in I Corps, a hundred and ten degrees with a ruck on."

Twenty minutes later, looking like something fished out of a sump pump, Smith walked into the VA hospital in Jamaica Plain and told the nurse at the desk he was having a nervous breakdown.

"Uh-huh," she said absently, not looking up from her log, pushing forward a stack of intake forms as dense as a small phone book. "Have a seat and fill these out, and listen up for your name when they call it out."

"Hey, lady, didn't ya hear me, I'm a 'Nam vet and I'm freakin' out!" Smith croaked. "I need to see a doctor and get me a shot a' somethin' fast!"

"Hey *yourself*," she harrumphed, peering over her wire rims in amused contempt. "Don't you see all these people here ahead of you? You *can* see, can't you? If not, make an appointment with the staff optometrist. He comes in on Tuesday and Friday."

She waved him on to a waiting room that was better than two-thirds full, an agglomerate of old, gray men who looked as if they had been parked there since Pearl Harbor. Several hours passed before Smith was shown in to see a young internist, who stopped him in mid-recitation to send him down the hall for a set of X rays. Finally, late that afternoon, Smith got in to see a staff psychiatrist, who listened with apparent interest as Smith retailed his years of terror. When he was done, however, the psychiatrist handed him—what else?—a scrip for Valium, and thoughtfully booked him for a follow-up visit three and a half weeks in the offing.

"Three and a half weeks!" Smith shouted. "I can't wait that long, man—they'll be fishin' me outta the Charles!"

"I'm sorry, Mr. Smith, that's the next available appointment. Should we call you if there's a cancellation?"

Ten years later, smacking his forehead in outrage, Smith says that it was almost as if the doctor was daring him to do it, to go home and take the gun down and stick the barrel between his teeth. "Over the years, I've talked to hundreds, maybe thousands, of 'Nam vets, and so many of 'em have said the same thing to me about the VA—it's like they *want* you to kill yourself, it's cost-effective medicine. Just please go have the decency to do it off the premises. It might, you know, give some of the doctors there PTSD if they hadda watch you do it."

Indeed, that sentiment, or something very like it, was expressed by a number of the men in Smith's shelter.

"You could see it in their eyes whenever you walked

through the door there—'Oh, boy, here's Quinlan again, that crazy fuck; why doesn't he just off himself already and quit wasting tax dollars?'" says Warren Quinlan, the former director of operations at the shelter. "In fact, I *begged* them to kill me, I pleaded for a lethal injection, anything to get out of the terrible [psychic] pain I was in. Their response was, 'We don't do that kinda thing around here,' which translates to, 'Go home and do it yourself, you lousy, rotten coward.'"

Mickey, a survivor of Khe Sanh, says he tried repeatedly to oblige the VA by killing himself. Once, after a week-long scotch-and-smack jam, he got into his car and purposely drove it, doing fifty-five, into the side of a building. "I've had last rites pronounced over me on three separate occasions, and *still* couldn't get the job done," he recalls. "But there were other guys I knew who didn't have that problem. One of 'em, my roommate at the West Haven VA, hung himself in the room there after they just ignored him for six months. Needless to say, that just did *wonders* for my recovery, coming back from a long day of group and AA to find him hanging there from a bedsheet."

What separates men like Mickey from the tens of thousands of 'Nam vet suicides is, to be sure, a vexed and open question. Suffice it to say that the line can't be drawn neatly between those who had happy childhoods and those who did not, nor are good jobs and loving families especially useful predictors. In the end, it may track to something as nebulous as *will*, which in Smith, at least, is as observable as his catalytic rage. For a year after his scandalous reception at the VA, he ran around the city looking for help, getting nowhere with several different private psychiatrists, whose dispassion he found baffling and insulting.

And then one day, driving down Commonwealth Avenue between EMS calls, Smith passed a storefront with a silhouette of a chopper over the door. Curious, he went inside and found himself in the Brighton Veterans' Center, a community-based drop-in clinic for vets in need of counseling. Staffed for the most part by fellow veterans with at least a modicum of clinical training, the Vet Center system (which now numbers more than two hundred units across the country) represents the single humane piece of programming put in by VA planners in the twenty-two years since the war. Free of the chaos and anomie of VA hospitals (but without either the beds or the manpower to house homeless vets), the centers have been, by and large, modest successes, commendable mainly for the sort of people who come to work there as counselors. One of them is John Wilder, a savvy, self-effacing former Marine, who came out of his office that day in 1985 to shake hands and sit down with Smith. Nine years later, Smith and his partners, Peace Foxx and Mark Helberg, will tell you that Wilder did no less than save their lives, and serve as the model for what to do with those lives once reclaimed.

"What John taught me, and what I've been able to pass on to the other vets here, is the power of validation—letting each guy know that their feelings are normal, considering what kind of hell they went through in the 'Nam," says Foxx, who, with George Mendoza, runs the combat support group at the shelter. A tall, soft-spoken black man with a thatch of gray hair and the gravity of a parish priest, Foxx is among the last people you'd associate with combat trauma, but in 1985, when he came in to see Wilder, he was on the verge of killing himself. He had a good job at the phone company and a big house in Dorchester, and must have looked, to anyone who knew him at the time, like an inner-city success story. But at home, in a room that he'd painted completely black, he'd sit alone with a tall scotch and a couple of grams of coke, wishing himself back to 'Nam. His marriage was falling apart, his two kids were barely talking to him, and at work, he was so alienated from the rest of the staff that he brooded about walking in one day and opening up with an M-16.

"Frankly, the only thing that saved me then was that I hated guns and never kept one around; otherwise, at the very least, I'd've taken myself out," he says. "It felt like there was no other way out for me, I was totally cut off from everyone, most of all from my wife and kids. I'd been to two different VAs and gotten no help at all from them, even though I told them that if they didn't do something, I was gonna kill myself or somebody else. But when I got in with one of the psychiatrists there, all he wanted to talk about was my childhood, or what was going on at home with my marriage. Meanwhile, memories of the 'Nam kept coming up, the booze and that whole routine weren't working anymore. There was this one memory I kept having about Rat Patrol, where you go out in a jeep with an M-60 mounted on it and comb the roads at night with no lights on. One night, we killed two gooks in a firefight and strung 'em to the back of the jeep with barbed wire. Back at the compound, I remember watching someone cut their ears and toes off, borrowing another guy's blade to do it because his own was too dull. All these years, I was constantly haunted by that image, watching the guy do it, but I could never put a face to it. Then one night, as I was driving home from the PTSD group, it suddenly came to me that the guy doing the cutting was me. It was *me*, man, all that time; I didn't want to be that person so bad, I had blocked my own face out. I cried and cried that night, and talked about it in group the next time we met, and a couple of the guys told me that they had done it, too, that it was part of what you did to survive over there. You just did things and you didn't think about it, because if you thought long, you thought wrong, as they used to say. You just *acted*, you just did it, and worried about it later—only, for me, later didn't come till *much*, much later.

"Anyway, with John [Wilder], I finally found someone I could tell all this to; more than anything, he was a wonderful listener. Besides the group, I did three years of one-on-ones with him, and the more I poured out to him, the more I kept remembering. A lot of times, it wasn't even stuff that I'd done, just things I'd seen happen that messed me up, like the time I was visiting a buddy of mine on post, and three mama-sans came running up to us with a bag over their shoulders. We yelled, 'Stop, stop!' but they kept coming at us and screaming, and we were about to open up on them when they stopped and threw the sack down and three dead babies rolled out. Man, those kids couldn't've been more than six months old, with blood and shrapnel wounds all over their bodies, and while me and the other guy were just standing there gaping, the mama-san yells out, 'You pay us money [for the dead children]!' I told that to John and I cried and then I probably cried some more, and he told me what he always told me, 'It's all right, man. Go ahead—you're *supposed* to feel this way. This is exactly how human beings have always reacted when they're put through the trauma you were.' Hearing that over and over again was the beginning of my redemption, how I got back the part of me I lost in Vietnam. My conscience, my moral nature, which I went against in 'Nam—John brought it out of hiding, or wherever it was, and put me back together again."

Smith, who was the last of the three partners to join the group, is no less rapturous about Wilder. "John, to me, is the soldier I grew up worshiping, the kind that does everything and takes credit for nothing. Every Wednesday night—*bang!*—at 6:59, eight murderous sons of bitches would come pounding through that door, and by 7:01, we'd all be at each other's throats—and somehow, not only did he get most of us better, he kept us all from killing each other, which is the *real* fuckin' miracle. I mean, every week, the group would lock and load on someone, push 'em over what we called the Angry Bridge straight into the Land of Sorrow. And believe me, if it was your turn, you'd be kickin' like a bastard—'Fuck *all* of you, I ain't goin' there, I'm *angry*, not sad—and after an hour, you'd be sittin' there bawling your ass off, and everybody'd get real quiet and let you grieve it till you were done with it."

"No, it wasn't a very pleasant thing to have to sit through for two hours, but hell, I mean, we were grunts—how else did we know how to do things?" says Helberg, the shelter's chief financial officer. "But what made it work, I think, was that John was so good at cooling guys out, not just stoking them up. Yeah, he'd push you to feel all these feelings that you'd been stuffing down, but when it got too hot in there and guys were jumping in each other's faces, John could dial it down without making anyone look stupid. Actually, now that I think about it, he was mostly refereeing between Kenny and somebody, because Kenny was always instigating, pushing other guys to give things up. Anything to keep the focus off of *him* and his feelings, because when it comes to things like feelings, Kenny doesn't like to give up shit."

Visited in his new office at the Vet Center in Worcester, Massachusetts, Wilder is amused to hear these descriptions of the group. "The truth, of course, is that it was exactly the opposite—I had to break my back to get *any* feelings out of them at all." He laughs. "I mean, *internally*, I'm sure they felt like their heads were going to explode, but outwardly, I was lucky if I got even a trickle of it from them.

"Understand that you're talking about guys to whom even a little rage is terrifying, after they saw what kind of damage that rage could do in Vietnam. But what I think I got across to them, both through talking about it and in diagrams, was that their rage had a very different job to do over there. When you're in a life-threatening situation like an ambush or a firefight, there's a section of the brain stem called the limbic system which overrides the cognitive mind and makes instant decisions for you. Basically, its function is to make sure the organism survives, and in giving up control to it, you can wind up doing some pretty awful things.

"But what I showed the guys in group was that they could turn that system *off* now, that in non-life-threatening situations like a fender-bender or an argument, they could talk to that part of the brain, say things to it like, 'Hey, man, it's okay, I got it this time; I might need you the next time, or the time after that, but I think I can manage from here.' Once they took that in, and saw that they *had* some control—so much control, in fact, that they were literally choking on their rage—*then* I think maybe they relaxed a little and let it out a bit. But it was never like they remember it, an Irish bar brawl in here. Believe me, if it had been, I'd've been the first one under the table."

Wilder laughs his halting, circumspect laugh, disavowing any claims to false bravery. A pale, mild man in a dark blue pullover, he looks like he'd be more at home behind the counter of a hardware store than fixing broken souls. But take a look at his résumé, and you'll find that the timid act doesn't wash. Along with a master's in psychology, it reveals fifteen years of treating a Who's Who of hard-cores: four years on an acute psych ward at the Bedford VA, handling the out-and-out crazies; two in heavy lock-down with the murderers at Walpole; and the last eight years in Vet Centers, where, as he reluctantly acknowledges, some of his clients come in armed and loaded. "It's one of the two rules I set—no weapons in group, period—but what am I gonna do, pat 'em down, do a strip search? I'm sure I'd never see most of them again, and even the ones I did would find ways to bring that stuff in. These guys are zen masters at the art of concealment—weapons, feelings, you name it."

A 'Nam-era enlistee, Wilder volunteered to serve in-country but wound up staying home and pushing papers instead. "Probably just as well," he says, playing the coward again, "because I never would've made it. Like I always tell these guys when they try to include me in their number, 'Hey, if I'd gone over there, I'd've fought with two stewardesses and three airline chairs,' because they'd've had to drag me off the plane holding on to them for dear life, and I wouldn't have let go the entire year. That's why I have so much respect for these guys, because they went in my place, and paid a heavy price for doing it. But if I treat somebody for two years, I have to tell them five times—*I wasn't there, so stop giving me credit for it.* They try so hard to include you, you know, to hold on to that us-versus-them thing, which is all part and parcel of the limbic encoding. It's very primal stuff back there, a lot of memories and impulses that they'll probably never reintegrate, no matter how hard they work at it. As much as they're trying to live in the here-and-now, part of 'em'll always be back in the bush there, pinned down under fire.

"I mean, why, for example, do so many of them hang out only with 'Nam vets? You ask them, they all say the same thing to you—'Hey, man, I need someone to watch my back.' Why would that still be important to them? Because that part of the brain, which is too primitive to reckon time, thinks that Vietnam happened *yesterday*, not twenty-five years ago, and that shots could ring out again at any second. The other piece of that is that when survival's at stake, the limbic system can't tell where you end and the next guy begins. I'd be rich if I had a buck for every time someone said in group, 'God, I *knew* it was me that caught that bullet in the chest, but it was actually Billy next to me in the hootch.' That's the real brilliance of military training, taking all these archaic impulses and getting them to act in concert, making each guy basically an extension of the next guy's sensory equipment. What's even more amazing is how these guys can spot each other in a crowd. Twenty years [after 'Nam], they'll point to a perfect stranger on the street and say, 'He was *there*, man; he *knows*'—and almost always, they're right."

Here I interrupt Wilder, still puzzled by the gap between his recollections and the group's. How, I ask, could those sessions have been so curative if all they elicited was a trickle of feeling in these men?

"Well, remember that for those guys, a trickle is a flood; after 'Nam, very few of them'll ever be criers and weepers. But that doesn't mean they couldn't process a lot here; they did. All of them, for instance, had a long history of nightmares. They brought them in, talked them out with one another, and fairly soon, the nightmares went away. Same deal with sleep disturbances—the vast majority of Vietnam combat vets have just terrible trouble sleeping. For twenty years, they've been waking up at two in the morning and not been able to get back to sleep, or they've laid there all night till five in the morning, and finally dropped off a couple of hours before the alarm. We talked about it in detail, and once again, I took them through the brain chemistry. I told them that if you've been badly traumatized before the age of twenty-five, when a certain part of the locus coerullus nerve mylenates, you get an extra batch of a stimulant called neuroprinefrine just before you fall asleep. They heard that, and again you could see the light come on in their eyes— 'Ahh, so it's *normal*, I'm *not* nuts; *everyone* in here has that.' It helped put an end to the major terror in their lives, which was the fear of going crazy, of losing it big-time. Once that was off their backs, they really began making some strides in here, letting go of a lot of the garbage they'd been carrying around since 'Nam.

"For instance, guilt. We went back and forth for months on this business of false responsibility, taking the blame for the death of a buddy when you couldn't've done anything to stop it. I explained to them that what they were *really* trying to do was keep that buddy alive, holding on to him in their head so that he wouldn't abandon them for good. Finally, though, I just had to get brutally blunt with them. I said, 'Look, I think you're all being incredibly selfish, holding on to those poor guys when what they really want from you is a burial.' That was *very* hard to take in, and I'm sure a lot of 'em hated my guts for it. But at some point, it must've gotten heard, I guess, because they stopped bringing in so many symptoms—the guilt dreams, the obsessive memories, all that stuff.

"Of course, they'd've probably gotten there sooner if we'd done things like stage mock funerals, but to be honest with you, I wasn't bright enough to think of it at the time. In fact, I wasn't bright enough to think of a *lot* of things at the time, which is why I start wincing whenever Kenny refers to me as his 'savior.' I mean, part of me is flattered that they hand me all the credit, but I'm not stupid enough to actually believe it. My guess is that they need to keep me alive in their heads, to refer to me as some sort of ongoing presence in their lives. That's fine, and I'll always be here for them, whether it's tomorrow or twenty years from now.

"But I want it clearly understood that *they* were the story, not me; it was their determination to get better that drove us forward, not some so-called brilliance of mine. In fact, if anything, they probably got better *in spite of me*, because most of the time, I really had no idea what I was doing. I stupidly insisted, for instance, on opening up the group to new guys, mainly because I couldn't say no to someone who'd had a leg blown off there. Quite rightly, Kenny and Mark and the others would bitch like crazy, saying it was disruptive and invasive and what the hell was the matter with me, anyway? But invariably, they'd take the new guy under their wing and teach him everything I'd taught them, and make the connection that, Aha, this was *me* ten months ago; I really *am* a long way up the road from where I started.

"You know, in retrospect, maybe that was how they figured out they had something valuable to offer, because after a year, year and a half, I was totally needless in that room. They'd blown by me on the rail and knew even more than I did—and so I came in one night and just fired them. Told them all to go out there and get on with it, already. Find out whatever it was that life had in mind for them."

HERE, THE STORY GENERALLY ENDS FOR WILDER'S clients. Most of them go back to what's left of their lives and try to reclaim those parts of it that are still salvageable: relationships with grown children who are at least as gun-shy as forgiving; credit ratings with banks that are content to get back pennies, if nothing else, on the dollar. A few of these men, however, seize the chance to become "twice-born," in Erik Erikson's phrase, starting afresh at college or at another vocation in pursuit of some new vision of themselves. So it was for Smith and his two partners, who had already begun the business of self-reinvention when the combat group broke up. Smith cut down his hours as a medic, took courses at night school to become a nurse, and got married to a woman with whom he would have two children, his first serious relationship in twenty years. Foxx had also enrolled in night school, earning a degree in human services while working full-time for the phone company. And Helberg, who'd weaned himself from a protracted coke habit, tiptoed his way through a messy divorce and devoted himself fervently to his young daughter, Jennifer, who'd been the one light, he says, in those years of darkness.

But six months after the group broke up, Smith and Helberg did something that blew the doors off their modest dreams. To celebrate their graduation from the group in style, the two of them flew to Washington to see the Wall— and came back from it undone, they say, changed almost beyond recognition.

"It's embarrassing to admit this, but we went there as ignorant as tourists—as ignorant, in fact, as we were when we went over to 'Nam," says Helberg. "We thought, 'Hey, what the hell, we got *our* shit together, after twenty-something months of heavy therapy.' Uh-uh, friend, it doesn't work like that; those are just words until you've rucked up and been to the Wall. Any unfinished business you got, the Wall will pull it out of you. Any uncried tears, any buddies you haven't said good-bye to, you better get ready to do it there, 'cause that Wall knows, man. It *understands*, and trust me, you're not going anywhere till it's good and done with you."

Helberg is one of those vets who don't have a whiff of the war upon them. He comes to work polished and dapper each day in an earth-tone double-breasted, his pink face as smooth as pumiced sandstone after twenty-five years of rough strife. The first time I saw him, in fact, I mistook him for Smith's lawyer and began peppering him with questions about the terms of the building's lease. But several weeks later, when we finally sat down to talk, he pulled up his pant leg and showed me a long set of scars, a deep purple spiderwork from his shin to his thigh, where a grenade had sheared it to the bone.

"A lot of [the scarring] is from skin grafts, to try and save the lower leg," he says. "I was crouched over when I tripped the wire, so the knee and the legbone took the brunt of it; a couple of inches to the right, and the grenade would've blown my balls off, and put some nice, fat holes in my chest and stomach, too. As it was, the surgeon pulled a half-pound of hardware out of me, all these bent nails and pig iron that the Cong used to make their frags. After three months of operations—and one infection after another from the heat—they were about ready to say, 'Sorry, Mr. Helberg, but we're going to have to remove it.' But a day or two before they were going to rotate me to Japan, the leg miraculously started to heal and the skin grafts took. That was the *good* news; the bad news was that in two weeks, I was back with the Air Cav in Cu Chi, getting choppered into the deep shit and coming back with a Huey full of [body] bags. This was Tet of '69, and believe me, nobody was too impressed with my limp or my Purple Heart. At *that* point in the war, with grunts falling left and right, if your trigger finger was working, brother, you weren't considered wounded."

For symbolic reasons, he and Smith chose the Fourth of July weekend to fly down and see the Wall. What with last-minute jitters and a crawl through the bars for courage, they didn't get to the little park until about two in the morning. There was a gaggle of people still traipsing the grounds, mostly sightseers and voyeurs on the prowl for sobbing vets. Helberg remembers thinking how odd it was that so many tourists were out late—and then he took his first good look at the Wall, and doesn't remember thinking much of anything after that.

"Oh man, it just hit me all at once—the names and the faces of the guys up on there, my own reflection off the marble like a ghost coming through it—and then it hit me again even harder, and literally knocked me on my ass. I can't tell you what I saw next because I saw *everything*, my whole tour, just exploding out of that Wall. Stuff I'd forgotten about, stuff I was *glad* I'd forgotten about; all the things I thought I'd put behind me in group, and much more. On my 201 form [a detailed addendum to the 214], it lists more than sixty confirmed firefights, and I think every single one of them came back to me that night, including the worst one of all, in this little ville outside Cu Chi.

"We'd got caught out in an ambush and had to call in for backup, then *more* backup and *more* artillery, and by the time it was all over and done with, there were dead GIs everywhere. Eighteen-year-old kids with their heads blown off, all puffed up like inner tubes from being dead two hours in that heat. Then I saw the *other* side, the unbelievable slaughter, dead kids and farm animals blown to bits by our artillery, old people burned to death on the floor of their huts. And any of them that *weren't* dead sure got that way in a hurry, guys shooting 'em in the head or torturing them before they shot 'em, shoving sticks and bayonets in their wounds. You have to understand that we'd just taken eighteen dead, and a lot of the brothers just flat out lost their minds behind it, killing anything that wasn't wearing U.S. dog tags.

"As for me, I was wandering around in just a total daze, supposedly securing the area but doing nothing of the kind, just gaping with big, fat saucer eyes at all of the death on the ground. I'd been raised, you know, a real religious kid—altar boy, all of that, eight years of parochial school—and as I walked around that ville, stepping over the corpses of these incredibly young VC, all I can remember thinking was, How *could* you, God? How could you allow *that* to happen, and *that*, and *that*, and *that*? And as I'm walking along and seeing this, that voice is getting louder, until I come across the thing that fucked me up for twenty years. It was just outside this hut where we'd found a deep set of tunnels, and she must've been running to it when the incoming caught her—a woman cradling a baby, curled up around it to protect it but just covered, man, the both of them, with chunks of hot shrapnel. Man, I looked at that, I just stood there with my eyes locked on to it, and when I turned away and looked back, I saw the Virgin and the baby Jesus."

He breaks off abruptly, pressing his fists together with enough torque to hoist a piano. After several moments, he fumbles for a cigarette on his desk, lighting it with shaky fingers. "I tell you, man, that one image did more to fuck me up than all the other stuff there put together. It made me bitter and cold, and turned me into a druggie on the spot—speed, hash, but especially opium. And fifteen years later, when my daughter Jennifer was born, it destroyed me all over again. Every time I'd hold her, or go to change her diaper, this beautiful pink baby would turn into a dead gook baby, and I'd back away from her like there was a fucking bomb ticking underneath her. Sometimes, my ex would look at me in total disgust and say, 'You know, Mark, not for nothing, but that war was fifteen years ago. *Get over it, already!'"*

Helberg did, finally, he says—at the Wall. "Oh, God, I cried and I cried, man—I don't think I stopped till the sun came up. Kenny, too, shockingly. In fact, every now and then, I'd start to come up for air and see him on the ground there crying his eyes out, and that'd just set me off worse than ever. Finally, I came out of it, like I say, around day-break, and started looking around for Kenny. Across the way, I see him sitting at this little campfire with a bunch of guys, smoking a bone and shooting the shit with them. I go over, and there's maybe *thirty* of these guys wearing the 'Nam pins and badges, and Kenny's busy interrogating 'em, like he does to everyone. 'So where were *you* guys in-coun-try?' 'Oh, I was in Pleiku.' 'I was in Dakto.' 'Was it hot for you there?' 'Oh, *beaucoup* hot, man; Charlie most definitely had his shit squared away; many brothers died there.' 'And where do you guys live now?' They all look at each other a second. 'We live here,' one of 'em goes. 'Where, you mean in D.C.?' 'No, man, *here*. Right here. You're lookin' at our PX, and our enlisted men's club.'

"Well, Kenny just about has a baby. 'What!' he starts shouting, 'You guys are *vets* and you're homeless? You got a Bronze Star, he's got a Silver, and you're all sleeping under a fuckin' treeline? What the hell kinda country is this that its decorated heroes eat outta Dumpsters?' The guys look at each other again, like 'Who's *this* asshole?' and say, 'What, they don't got any homeless in *your* town?' 'Well, yeah, thousands of 'em,' says Kenny, 'but they're just bums and crackheads; we step over 'em in the street.' 'Yeah, well, you better step lightly, pal, 'cause a lot of those bums're grunts, and one of 'em just might reach back for some gusto on you.'"

Devastated, Smith and Helberg slunk back to the Wall and stood there glaring at it like a pair of spurned suitors. They'd come down here to take a victory lap not just for themselves but for their dead, to tell their brothers on the black marble that they hadn't died cheaply. Now that triumph seemed sodden and mean, to attach to no one but two selfish goldbricks from Boston. Guilt was like malaria in Vietnam: anyone who caught it was infected for life, and Smith and Helberg, who had it bad, now began to feel globally responsible. Maybe if you'd fought at Bataan or the Marne, you could separate out who you owed from who you didn't. But in a war as messy and anarchic as 'Nam, how could you begin to tell who'd taken a bullet for you, or flown the resupply bird that bailed out your unit? No, any way they cut it, it came out the same for Smith and Helberg: the men behind the treeline were as much their business as those up on the Wall, and after staring morosely at said Wall for several minutes, the two of them suddenly gaped at each other in shared epiphany.

"Kenny was the one who said it, I think, but he didn't even have to—both of us just *knew* at the exact same moment what we were going to do with the rest of our lives," says Helberg. "And what was even weirder was, usually when you get a flash like that, you charge off in five different directions at once, trying to make something happen before it goes away from you. But Kenny and I were completely calm, like, 'Fuck it, God has spoken; this *will* get done.'

"Unfortunately, as we found out over the next couple of years, God doesn't know anyone at the VA or the GAO [General Accounting Office]—or if He does, they weren't returning our phone calls. Not only were we totally on our own with this, we were so ignorant we didn't even know we were ignorant. Which, come to think of it, was probably the one thing we had going for us. If we'd had *any* idea how wacko this all was, trying to launch a veterans shelter in the middle of a recession without two bucks between us and no friends at City Hall—shit, we'd've gotten laughed out of our own *living rooms*, forget about down at the VA. Only we didn't *tell* the VA about it, didn't tell anybody about it; we just went out and made it happen, one tiny, little step at a time. And by the time people caught on to what we were doing, we were a big fucking tidal wave and *nobody* was laughing at us—least of all the VA."

IF WHAT FOLLOWS SOUNDS PREPOSTEROUS, A conflation of self-mythology, understand that what we are dealing with here is something singularly indomitable: three hacked-off grunts possessed of an honorable idea. However many things are wasted on the young, military training isn't one of them, and at the age of 18, Smith, Foxx, and Helberg had had it beaten into them that an honorable idea was worth dying for. They were further given to believe that no objective was beyond their grasp, that any hill could be taken with sufficient balls, smarts, and stealth. Once back in Boston, Smith and Helberg recruited Foxx over the phone, and the three of them went after it like a squad of star LURPs. They devoted a year and a half to intensive recon, going from shelter to shelter and alleyway to alleyway, counting veterans and culling their stories.

"At two in the morning, when you *really* see what's what in these places, we'd walk into hellholes like the Night Center in the theater district, and find mothers and little babies sleeping on folding chairs, and crazy drunks screaming and fighting each other," says Smith. "And way in the

back there, all by themselves, would be twenty vets in cam-
mies [camouflage outfits], two of 'em sittin' guard duty
while the other guys slept.

"We'd do whatever we could for those guys, get 'em
fed and cleaned up and put into the system. But after our
twentieth or twenty-fifth run to the VA—sitting down with
each of these guys and doing the paperwork to get them
admitted, then waiting around all day for 'em to try and
get seen—after, like I say, the twentieth time we lost a
day's pay to do this, only to have 'em spit out with a how-
de-do and that yellow thing of Valium, we said, 'Fuck it,
you bastards, we'll take care of it ourselves. It's obvious
you have no intention of taking care of these men, with
your $35-billion-a-year pork barrel and golf clubs.'"

Foxx and Helberg began running support groups wherever vets congregated, commandeering a room, for instance,
at the mammoth Long Island Men's Shelter and summoning
anyone with discharge papers. "They'd come down by the
dozens, holding out their 214, which had been folded and
unfolded so many times it was falling apart at the creases,"
says Helberg. "Most of these guys had nothing else to their
name, but you bet your sweet ass they still had that 'fourteen. It was like their last piece of proof that they'd *been*
somebody, that underneath the filth, they weren't bums,
they were *vets*. And, man, the way they'd hand it over to
you, like it was a sick animal—I tell you, that made me feel
like I was back at the Wall again, with all that hurt and sadness in me."

Obsessed, the three of them staked out the libraries,
reading everything they could get their hands on about
PTSD. They traveled around the country on their own thin
dime, compiling a database of homeless vets in cities like
L.A., San Diego, New York, and Detroit. And by the spring

of 1989, when their scout mission was done, they had considerably more than mere numbers to wave. At the drop of a hat, they could produce hundreds of homeless vets, who would march (or more likely, limp, in a shambling attempt at lockstep) on the VA or the governor's mansion. In old-boy Boston, where military service is still a distinction and the word *patriot* calls to mind more than just the football team in Foxboro, this kind of flag waving will get you noticed in a hurry, and in June, when Smith began paying calls on local politicians, it was with consummate awareness of his growing clout.

"I felt like I was the leader of this humongous gang, only *my* gang was ex-Marines, and Seals, and Army Rangers, and nobody wanted five hundred of *them* loitering outside their office," says Smith. "Plus, we were starting to get all this press about hometown heroes eating outta Dumpsters, and sleepin' with the fat rats in the Red Line tunnel, and who the hell wanted to be blamed for that? Of course, most of the major players tried to stiff us with promises, or whine about the recession or the Bush administration. But one guy who stepped right up to the plate was [Congressman] Joe Kennedy II, who wasn't even a vet. In fact, the first time I'd met him, back in '87, when he came to the combat group to ask for our votes, I'd ripped him a new asshole for bein' a rich-boy draft-dodger. But two years later, he's sitting on the Veterans Affairs Committee, and does everything in his power to help get us this building.

"In fact, it was Kennedy's aide who pulled me aside one day and told me to read the Stuart B. McKinney Act for the Homeless. In it, buried on page 137 or somewhere, was this provision that said that any government building that was either abandoned or underutilized had to be handed over to nonprofits for the homeless. A month later, we hand-delivered this application the size of the *Britannica* directly to the [General Services Agency's] headquarters in Maryland. We got in with Judy Brightman, the director of facilities management at Health and Human Services, and let her know we were serious as a heart attack about gettin' a building fast. 'It might be only August,' I said, 'but winter comes early in New England. Three months from now, guys'll be piling up on the coroner's table, blue-black frozen like a side a' steak—and most of 'em will have USMC tattooed across their shoulder.'"

Of course, it wasn't just any building that Smith and his partners were angling for. However steep its decline over the last couple of decades, 17 Court Street was a premium property, drawing bids of $20 million from private developers. None, it's safe to assume, admired its squat, gray lines, or affected the vaguest interest in its ninety-year history; what they saw was a piece of real estate around the corner from City Hall that they could pull down and replace with one of those forty-story cash registers. Not that Smith was any more sensible of the building's faint charms. What turned *him* on was that it had been a VA clinic for fifty years, where hundreds, perhaps thousands, of the men he represented had been seen and sent packing in a bureaucratic heartbeat. Nothing thrilled him more than the idea of sticking it to the VA, converting its dank quarters into a scene of hope and rebirth.

In their forays to Washington over the next several months, meeting with Vietnam combat vets like senators John Kerry of Massachusetts and Bob Kerrey of Nebraska, it occurred to Smith and Helberg that a heady change was in the air. The generation that fought that war had come of age politically, throwing off at last the encumbrance of silence to claim its due as men and warriors. Taking their inspiration from the Wall and their protocol from the recovery movement, Vietnam veterans' advocates all over the country were demanding that attention be paid, that steps be taken to repair both their honor and condition. Where but ten years ago, there'd been only a handful of such groups, now Smith could count between forty and fifty, and a coalition had sprung up among them to maximize influence and speak with one voice to power.

Back home in Boston, Smith detected the same sea change in progress. Old-line veterans groups like the DAV and the VFW, once so indifferent to Vietnam vets, threw their support behind the proposed shelter, offering everything from soup to staff. Cornerstone firms in the financial district, from whom Smith had expected vigorous opposition, put up not a peep of protest, though doubtless some of them were less than exalted, fearing drunks and thieves on their doorstep. But for Smith, the surest marker of a shift in attitudes was the ease with which he and his partners were able to raise money. One day, out of the blue, Smith dashed off a letter to David Mamet, asking the famous playwright for his help. Three days later, Mamet showed up on his doorstep, proclaiming to Smith and Helberg that he was "honored to be in the presence of such warriors." Before Mamet left that night, they extracted from him a promise to write them a play, the proceeds from which would be used to support the Vietnam Veterans Workshop, as their project had come corporately to be known.

Not content, however, to take yes for an answer, Smith, whose many defects do not include bashfulness, further prevailed upon Mamet to stage a benefit for them, featuring big-name talent from Hollywood. That fall, Mamet obliged with a coup de theatre, directing Al Pacino, Michael J. Fox, Christopher Walken, and Lindsay Crouse in an extraordinary evening called *Sketches of War*. The must-see event of the season in Boston, *Sketches* fetched a standing-room crowd at the Old Colonial and raised a quarter of a million dollars in two hours. It also made Smith et al. the pet cause of the power crowd, who were delighted to dig deep for such close, personal friends of Mamet's. In charity, as in show business, nothing succeeds like success, a lesson Smith has since put to prodigious use.

"A lot of nonprofits try to shake you down with guilt, saying, 'Oh, isn't this horrible, how can we allow this as a society?' Well, excuse me, but nobody wants to hear from that kinda shit. What they want to hear is that you've got a program that actually *works*, that changes the situation for good and forever. People come in here, see 350 vets busting their asses—shoveling down dinner to get to their computer programming class, or make the six o'clock AA meeting, or their sit-down with the financial planning guy—people see that, and they start reaching for their checkbooks. That's why, when all the other nonprofits are treading water, my operating budget's growing one hundred percent a year, and I'm adding staff and programs so fast I can hardly keep up with it. That's why HUD's given me $8 million to rebuild this place, and another $5 million to build SROs across town. That's why grants keep pouring in from the Department of Labor and Social Security—because they know they get a huge bang for every buck they put in here.

"Let me tell you a secret about homelessness in America—it's turned into a cozy little business for a lot of people. The money's not bad, especially at the executive level, and nobody expects a goddamn thing from you; just keep *some* of those crazy bastards off the streets at night, and maybe mop the shelter out once or twice a week. Where's the incentive to fix the problem when you're gettin' forty bucks a head a night, and there's no one pokin' around asking what you're actually accomplishing with that money? Bottom line, it's just a job for most of these people, a ho-hum nine-to-five. Why strain yourself and stick around till 5:01—those drunks ain't goin' anywhere. Well, some of those drunks are my brothers, pal, and this ain't my job, it's my mission—a red-hot op to bring 'em all back home. There's half a million vets out there, what I call our stateside MIAs, most of 'em the sick and wounded from 'Nam—and neither me or Mark or anyone else here is gonna quit until the last one is present and accounted for."

ON JANUARY 2, 1990, WITH A SIX-MONTH, $1-A-year lease in hand, Smith and his two partners turned the key in the lock at 17 Court Street—and walked in on an unspeakable shambles. Like the South Vietnamese army deserting Hue City, the VA had left its stark wreckage everywhere. Hallways were impassable with big junk and bed frames. Fixtures had been ripped down and the plumbing sabotaged, and almost every window in the place had been broken from the inside, letting in deep piles of snow. There was neither heat in the building nor lights and only one working toilet—but such was the program's juice on the street that by noon, 150 homeless veterans had trooped in to help.

"They were cold and sick and had so much snow in their beards, they looked like dime store Santas—but fuckin'-A, they were ready to work," says Smith. "I gathered 'em all into one big circle over there, and held my first-ever town meeting. I said, 'Brothers, I know it looks like hell in here, but this place is *home* and no one's takin' it away from us. The question is, how're we gonna live in our home? Are we gonna treat it like shit, the way people have treated us? Or are we gonna treat it like we *should've* been treated from day one, with the respect and honor we earned as soldiers? I *want* that respect, I fought my heart out for this country. If you want it, too, let's make this a home that we're proud of. *Then* maybe we'll start gettin' the respect we all deserve."

For the next hour, stodgy Court Street was treated to a most peculiar tableau: 150 ragged, unbathed men scrounging for mops, pails, brooms, cleanser, hammers, nails, and plywood. By five o'clock, the building's broken windows had been covered and a clearing cut into the deep stand of garbage. Smith looked around and, though it was scarcely less dark or frigid inside than it was out on the street, declared the New England Shelter for Homeless Veterans ready and open for business.

CHAPTER THREE

JACK'S HUGE LEGS WRESTLE EACH OTHER UNDER-neath the chair, and his arms intertwine like a pair of prize boas, crossing and uncrossing at his chest. There are men in this building who give off rage so redolent you can track it from a block away. Others emanate such guilt or grief that your clothes fairly reek of it afterward. But with Jack, what you smell is the funk of blind panic, and the scent is over-powering today.

"I—I've been gettin' ready to tell you about this all week," he quavers. "I can see it so good now, I even remember what we ate that day, and what the air smelled like on the beach."

He gulps, scrunching himself into a cumbrous ball, his big, sweet face going as red as a goal light. He has actually been getting ready to tell me this for a month, but each time he got to the story of Daring Rebel II, a raid of two hundred Marines on a barrier island near Da Nang, his stomach seized up and the shakes got so bad, we had to end the session amidships. Yesterday, however, he got halfway through it in therapy, and today, with his therapist beside him, he is determined to gut through the rest of it, and break the twenty-year choke-hold of this memory.

"The Navy Seals went in first and cleared the beach for us, then we came in off the BLT [Battalion Landing Team troop ship] and set up a position," he begins. "We torched the whole ville, like we always did, and pushed everything into a pile with the bulldozers. Then"—he breaks off, his jaw beginning to rattle like a rock slide—"then we had target practice with their animals. Chickens, pigs, goats, cattle—it was all those people had in the world, and we slaughtered it up for fun. You know what happens when you nail a dog with an M-16 round? It *explodes*, there's nothing left of it but the head and some fur, and these guys thought that was about the funniest thing in the world. Them poor animals're screamin' and runnin' for their lives, and these sick fucks are after 'em, laughin' their heads off. . . ."

He is already weeping and contorting himself, a grotesque, untutored yoga. Leslie Lightfoot, his therapist, leans in to talk to him in a voice that is both a command and a caress. "Let it out, Jack, don't stop yourself; there's nothing shameful about an honest emotion. Forget the war story, go with the *feeling*; that's all that matters in here."

Jack weeps as per ordered, in the choked cadence of the unpracticed; Marines cry about as often as they blow retreat. Then, like the good and faithful soldier he is, he gathers himself bolt upright and continues. "Someone found a map, it showed that the [village] cemetery was an ammo dump, so we started in digging it up. I got about four feet down when I hit something solid with my E-tool, accidentally busted it open. . . . Inside was the body of a real old lady with long, gray hair, and when my shovel hit the box . . . it knocked her head off her shoulders—*it jumped out at me in the hole!*" Jack breaks off, sobbing. "I got so wicked, wicked sick, I ran off to the side of the hill to throw up, and the LT—do you believe it?—ordered us all to break for chow!"

He stops again, hugging his gut with both arms, suppressing the dry nausea in his throat.

"Do you want to quit, Jack? Let's stop it right here—no one says you have to finish today," says Lightfoot.

"No! I *wanna* finish, I want it *outta* me!" he bellows. "It's been fuckin' up my life for goddamn ever. . . ."

"Fine," she says firmly, "but just remember, it's your call. MACV [Military Affairs Command Vietnam] isn't running your life anymore."

He grunts, resenting her dig at his fierce loyalty. He'd given everything to the Marine Corps in Vietnam, and when that wasn't enough, he'd given for his family, as well, re-upping in-country for a couple of half-tours so that his ungrateful brothers could stay home. He'd come back to the States hating MACV as much as he'd ever hated the Cong, but for all the brute savagery of his buddies on that island, his love for the Corps was untainted. As any Marine will proudly tell you, there is no finer example of brainwashing on the planet than what takes place at Parris Island.

"A lotta the guys were laughin', walking around with skulls on their E-tools," he continues. "They got a kick outta mockin' the bodies, throwin' their empty C-rats into the graves, and pissin' and spittin' on top of 'em. There were bodies hangin' offa tank turrets and guys stringin' 'em from PCs [personnel carriers] like they were all such beaucoup tough motherfuckers. I've laid in bed all night for years thinkin' about that, try'na justify the sacrilege, and I can't. To me, that's why we lost the goddamn war, 'cause we fought like animals and made everybody there hate us. We were s'posed ta been heroes, a country that fought by the rules, and instead, we killed their goats and pigs, and dug up people's grandparents. . . ."

Another round of sobs rolls in, like a long set of waves

at dusk. Lightfoot sits there, impassive, letting his grief undo itself and die. When the room is quiet again a moment, she says, "Is there anything you'd like to tell those villagers if they were here with us today?"

Jack looks up and nods with great, avid relief. "I'd tell 'em all I'm sorry from the bottom of my heart. Nobody *made* us desecrate corpses, or shoot up all those animals. Myself, I coulda checked my fire, but I didn't. . . ."

"Are you sure about that, Jack?" presses Lightfoot, gently. "What do you think would've happened if you *hadn't* shot those animals, or if you'd intentionally shot over their heads?"

Having plunked himself down in the old wallow of guilt, Jack looks up, sorely discomfited. "What do you mean by that?"

"I mean, what would've happened with the guys in your unit if you hadn't pulled the trigger that day?"

"I—I dunno. I guess maybe they'd have lost faith in me. Thought that I'd turned on 'em, or somethin'."

"And isn't that faith in each other what they beat into you in boot camp, and what kept you guys alive in the jungle?"

"Yeah, but—"

"So you *had no* choice, did you, Jack?" she puts in firmly. "You had to do your job, there was no option. You couldn't've been a saint and made it home."

He sags in his chair, gaping at her, pinned fast by the steel tip of the truth. "No. I guess not," he murmurs. "I—I always thought I was spineless, I had no heart to stand up to 'em. . . ."

"I got news for you, Jack: so did all those kids walking around that day with skulls on their shovels. And don't think they're in any less agony about it than you. If they weren't, there wouldn't be a quarter-million of 'em on the streets tonight."

ONE YEAR AGO, ON THE SORT OF WARM SPRING day that feels like the commutation of a long jail sentence, Jack got on the C-line in downtown Boston and took it five stops to Kenmore Square. A block between the Square and Fenway Park, there is an overpass forty feet or so above the Massachusetts Turnpike. A little before five o'clock, Jack climbed the fence of the overpass and looked down at the four-lane Pike, which was already abuzz with outgoing traffic. Measuring the drop, however, it occurred to him that unless he dove headfirst, a fall from this height wouldn't suffice to kill him, which meant that the actual instrument of death would be some poor bastard's front bumper. This troubled Jack enormously, as did everything else about his life, not least his stunning incompetence at ending it. In the course of the last twenty years, he'd tried everything from pills to car exhaust, but inevitably fudged the dosage, or left a rear window ajar. A thoroughly decent man whose only cruelty was reserved for himself, he couldn't bear the thought of saddling a stranger with his death—but neither could he bear the thought of climbing down from the fence.

If there were an electroencephalograph that recorded psychic pain, Jack's reading would have staggered the needles that day. In a two-year nose-dive, he'd lost everything he had in the world, including the faint hope that he'd one day get any of it back. His marriage and the two kids he loved so dearly; the house with the big pool and basketball court that he'd worked around the clock to finance; the car, the job, the barest sufficiency of self-respect—all of it out the window in one withering speed rush. With it went the last

check on his importunate memories—the corpses of the Viet
Cong stacked up like kindling in Da Nang; the stench of the
green stretchers he'd had to hose down before missions,
sloughing the blood of his buddies off the canvas. Worse
than any of that, though, was the lunatic racket in his ears,
the product of a fluky accident in Da Nang. As chief of an
artillery crew on Hill 41, Jack was fishing a dud round out
of a mortar when it discharged and nearly took his head off
with it. Blown twenty feet off the parapet, the right side of
his scalp on fire, he'd awoken in an evac two days later in
the vise of the most mind-fucking pain. The pain eventually
subsided, with a lot of help from booze and morphine, but
what remained, impervious to all medication, was a wailing
in both ears like a car alarm. Over the years, he'd been to see
a battery of doctors, including the VA audiologist who suggested, with perfect seriousness, that Jack go through life
wearing a Walkman tuned between stations. No, the only
thing that turned down the volume in his head was a long
hit off a crack pipe—and then another, and another, until
he'd smoked himself into a frenzy, and there was nothing
left for him to do but climb that fence.

As he looked down at the turnpike, he got more dis-
traught by the minute. This was the worst kind of death,
bereft of honor and sanctity, but coming over there, he'd
wanted to die in the worst kind of way. Since the spring of
1991, when his wife kicked him out of the house, he'd
bounced from one VA hospital to another, desperate to find
someone who'd actually *listen* for once and not fob him off
with drugs. At the Causeway VA, though, he never saw the
same psychiatrist twice, and at Brockton, where he went for
a simple outpatient reference, the young intern panicked
and rang the bell for security. Dumbstruck, Jack turned to
leave and was gang-tackled by the guards, who fogged and

choked him with aerosol Mace and dragged him upstairs to the "seclusion ward." That, at any rate, is what the VA calls it; vets who've done time there know it better as the Flight Deck, where for most of four months Jack was kept flying, all right, stacked up on so much Haldol and Trylophon that he was jumping out of his skin in slow motion. There were ten other 'Nam vets on the ward, he says, and whenever one of them let out an honest emotion about the war, the doctors upped his dosage and tacked on two weeks to his stay. In short order, Jack learned to keep his mouth shut tight, to do his time in silence and get out.

"What kills me is how the VA tells you everything's changing over there, gettin' better for Vietnam vets—but this happened to me *just last year*," he seethes. "In fact, seems like every time I went to them for outpatient therapy, whether it was at Brockton or Jamaica Plain or this building here when it was VA, I wound up on a gurney in four-point leather restraints. That's why, even when I'd go see private shrinks, I never, ever talked to 'em about the 'Nam—I was afraid they'd hit that button under their desk and call the cops on me. Meanwhile, I had so much stuff backed up, so much pain and fear and nightmares in me, that I'd grab the fuckin' bedpost in my sleep and squeeze it till it was all deformed. Ask my ex, it's one of the things she always screamed at me for, ruinin' that bed frame of hers. Three posts on it were all straight and normal—and the fourth one was like twisted into the shape of my hands, hangin' on for dear life or something."

About the ex-wife and her complaints, considerably more later; sadly, you cannot tell the story of these men without talking about the bitterness they've sown, if for no other reason than because the bearers of that bitterness are gaining on them every second. The punitive ex-wives, bringing lawsuits and assault charges; the grown or teenage children acting out with a vengeance, tracking their addictions and arrest records all over the house—for most vets, it never ends and there is nowhere to run from it. Indeed, in treatment, as therapists like Lightfoot can tell you, Vietnam often gets bumped to the end of a long line of life issues, and it can be weeks or months working your way back to it.

"Vietnam vets are crisis junkies, they can't walk away from it," says Lightfoot. "One week, it's their sixteen-year-old daughter getting knocked up, the next, it's the twenty-year-old drinking his way through his rent money—and how do you say to the vet, 'Yeah, but forget about all that, let's concentrate on *you* for a while.' They've got terrible guilt, especially where their kids are concerned, and it just kicks in with the old survivor guilt: 'How can I move on with *my* life when my kids are stuck in hell?' It's this high-wire juggling act you're constantly doing, treating the 'Nam stuff and the family stuff and everything in between, because any one piece of it, if you leave it alone, could knock him off that wire. And when these guys fall, it's a long way down. Some of them, you never see back here again."

As it happened, Lightfoot had seen Jack only hours before he climbed the fence last year. In and out of the shelter after his stay at the Brockton VA, he walked into her office that day looking like a well-fed zombie and told her he was upset about his son. She took one peek at the shopping bag he brought in with him, which was full of VA sedatives and antipsychotics, and concluded it would be very slow going with him. That evening, however, she got his call from the overpass. He was absolutely, definitely going over the rail, he said, unless somebody did something for his boy.

"What with all the meds Jack was on at the time, I'd missed how broken up he was about Nicky," says Lightfoot. "The two years he was out of the house, his kid had had a real bad time of it, getting tossed out by the mother and bouncing around from a foster home to a reform school, where he was calling Jack every night and crying 'Help me, save me!' On the phone that day with Jack, trying to get him down off the fence, I promised him I'd go day and night with him on the PTSD stuff, and work toward getting him physical custody of the kid. That was all he needed, to hear that someone would finally pay him some *sustained* attention. He'd been looking all over town for it and never found it."

Curiously, one of the places Jack had applied for it was this shelter, where he'd lived and worked in two previous stints, and undertaken therapy with a couple of different people. "Ah, but that's what's so instructive about his case—that even here, in a program devoted to these guys, it took Jack three passes to get what he needed," says Lightfoot. "This is an art, not a science, and who knows why he didn't click with those other people. The point is, where a lot of vets give up and say, '*Fuck* the VA,' or '*Fuck* the shelter,' Jack kept pushing and found the right fit. And there isn't one guy out there—I don't care how damaged or pissed off—who can't be helped by the right clinician. All it takes is one, and this shelter doesn't have a monopoly on them. I know some wonderful people, in fact, who work at the VA and the Vet Centers."

None, it's safe to assume, are more revered than Lightfoot. Among men who would bad-mouth the Easter Bunny, you hear nothing but tone poems to her skill and savvy, and her "total dedication to the brothers." Few, if any, of them know that she does this work for nothing, that she has never accepted a dime to treat Vietnam veterans. It is a vow she took as a young medic in Germany, where thousands of grunts came through her ward, their souls compressed like scrap metal. She got home in 1970, earned a master's degree on the GI bill, and built a thriving practice in central Massachusetts. Seven years ago, she bought a detox facility in Leominster, freeing up the time to do pro bono work. And so, twice a week, she gets up at five in the morning to drive the ninety miles to the shelter. Because there are men backed up to see her, and because she is incapable of saying no to any of them, she invariably works through lunch each day and staggers out, punch-drunk, after ten solid hours of it.

"Yeah, it's a long day," she confides, nipping at the coffee in her lap, holding on to it like a handrail in a hurricane, "and not too many of these guys come in and take the session off, either, and bitch about their upstairs neighbors. But that's exactly why I love working with them, because they *don't* fuck your time off, or waste a month trying to get to the bottom of their resistance. They're in pain and it hurts and they want help now, and when they get it, they put it to good use and get on with their lives. People—other *therapists*, in fact—ask me, 'Isn't it depressing treating Vietnam vets?' No sir, what *you* do, treating Back Bay narcissists, is depressing. This stuff I find exhilarating."

Apparently, because whatever portion of her weekend that isn't devoted to her thesis on PTSD is spent writing grant proposals for a hospice she intends to open for Vietnam vets. "A lot of these guys came home with raging heroin habits," she says, "and almost inevitably, heroin means AIDS now. I don't know how many of them are dying out there in some rathole city hospital, but I know that there are a lot and even one is too many. Bad enough they were robbed of a life in that war. To have to die like that, anonymous, without an ounce of love and honor—I'm sorry, but I think this country's better than that. At least I hope to God we are."

SOMEONE ONCE SAID, APROPOS OF THE THE-ater, that the character who commands our interest onstage is the one undergoing great change. Indeed, change—or metamorphosis, more like it—is our sovereign national myth: immigrant to American, poor man to millionaire, ugly duckling to swan. It was with no small wonder and excitement, then, that I watched Jack transformed before my eyes by Lightfoot. Four months into treatment, he'd won physical custody of his son, thanks in large part to her testimony on his behalf in court. By October, he and the boy had moved into a two-bedroom apartment, cooing and squabbling less like father and son than a pair of reunited lovers. Gone was Jack's dead-eyed, hangdog look, and much of the beer gut he'd put on in the last five years, when he polished off a six-pack over dinner every night and another six parked in front of a game on the tube. Indeed, the guy who showed up now on the dot of ten for his twice-a-week sessions with Lightfoot was beginning to look a lot like the handsome drill instructor in his puckered snapshots from Lejeune.

One morning, he came in, spit-shined and barbered, and announced he'd been picked up the night before by a 19-year-old girl. "Do you believe it, she said I looked thirty-five." He giggled. "She musta had an aneurysm or something."

"That's *astigmatism*, Jack, and I'm not sure I approve of this," said Lightfoot. "You want to date a teenager, that's your funeral. But let's at least get you home from Da Nang first."

"Christ, what a hardass, this one," Jack groaned, rolling his eyes in mock exasperation. "A guy can't even get laid around here without gettin' rung up by her."

"No, Jack, you can get laid if you want to. For that matter, you can go to the track and put your kid's lunch money on the 'two' horse. But part of my job is to help you make better decisions, and at this stage, I don't think a nineteen-year-old's such a great call. Don't get me wrong, I'm delighted you're feeling better about yourself. But before you go catting around like a cadet on shore leave, I think we've got some business to attend to. As I recall, you were having a real hard time yesterday with the Vietnamese farmer you shot."

Jack grunted and bent over, staring at his shoe tops, the lightness of the moment dissolved. "All last night, too; I couldn't stop thinkin' about him. Is it ever gonna go away?" he croaked.

"Yes, he will, Jack, absolutely; you're halfway there already. Remember, you couldn't even *talk* about him until a couple of weeks ago. When we've gotten you through the grief of it, and you've had all your other feelings, too—your anger at the LT for ordering you to take him out; your regret for his family, who you didn't know was right there watching it—once we've brought you through all of that, it'll lose its power to haunt you. That I promise."

"What, it's just gonna blow away and disappear?" he asked skeptically.

"No, it'll always be there somewhere, and come back to you from time to time. But when it does, it'll be just a memory, not an accusation. You'll have made your terms with it."

Jack swallowed, shut his eyes, and began wiping his

hands on his pants, damping down the creases compulsively. "I—I wasn't even aimin' at him, you know, I was aimin' at the water buffalo alongside a' him," he begins. "He was no more than ten yards in front of the highway and we're all yellin', '*Dong lau! Dong lau!*' and, meanwhile, our convoy's maybe a quarter-mile up the road. If he'da made it onto the highway with that buffalo a' his, and the convoy'd had to stop to go around them two, a sniper with an M-60 coulda wiped the whole unit out. At least, that's what the guys in my platoon were tellin' me afterwards. . . ."

"But you didn't believe them?"

"*No*, I didn't believe them," Jack bawled, punching his thigh. "He was just an old man with his water buffalo and his kids, and the Cong don't ambush nobody with their kids hangin' around 'em."

He broke off, weeping in short, tight bursts, holding down the noise as best he could. He'd reconciled himself, in the last several weeks, to the rank necessity of tears, but he was damned if he was going to let some prick across the hall overhear it. For Jack, there was too much of that going on around here in the first place, all this men's club sharing and crying on each other's shoulders. Sure, a lot of things were changing these days, and maybe some of them for the better—but who the fuck had gone and turned the Marines into the Oprah Winfrey show?

"I ran across the road, callin' for a corpsman," he resumed, "and outta nowhere, the old man's kids come runnin' up to me, punchin' and kickin' me in the gut, in the legs. Meanwhile, there's blood spurtin' outta this tiny hole in his chest, and his whole family's screamin' and hollerin' at me. I don't understand a word of it, and the guys in my platoon are clappin' me on the back, tellin' me what a big, fuckin' hero I am. All this stuff is goin' on, all this noise and scrambling, and someone's dragging me across the road and puttin' me onto a chopper, and even from over there, the only sound I hear is the sound of the old man dyin'. That death gurgle in his throat, like he was choking on his own blood—man, I just wanted to run right back to him and sit him up in my arms. Say, 'I'm sorry, mister, I'm sorry. *Please* don't die on me. . . .'"

Jack lurched up and staggered out the door in the direction of the bathroom. For several minutes, we heard the report of his dire, spasmic retching, but when I offered to go look in on him, Lightfoot told me to stay put and be quiet. "That's the first rule of trauma work—'Don't just do something; *sit* there,'" she said. "Jack's been waiting a long time to be rid of this stuff. The last thing he needs is you to pull him away from it."

When Jack returned, lacquered in a coat of clear sweat, he looked five pounds lighter and immeasurably relieved. "I know how you're always tellin' me, 'Get it up, get it outta you,'" he said sheepishly, "but I'm not sure if that's exactly what you had in mind."

"Hey, any way's a good way, as long as no one's bleeding," Lightfoot smiles. "How do you *feel* now, after all that?"

"Good, actually; a lot better, in fact. You know, in the bathroom, all this stuff started comin' back to me. I remembered that after I shot the old man, they sent me to the rear to get drunk for five days. I think maybe some a' what came outta me just now was the memory of all that booze. You wouldn't believe what all I was sockin' down back then. I was literally tryin' to drink myself to death."

"Well, a part of you was, anyway," said Lightfoot. "Do you think we can go back now and ask that part of you to at least consider whether the old man was VC?"

"Well, but I just finished tellin' you, Les, he didn't have a rifle or anything, and his whole family was right up behind him there—"

"Correction. His family didn't show up until *after* you shot him. At the time you pulled the trigger, you only knew what the LT told you—that he was a prime VC suspect and a danger to your brothers. To have thought otherwise would have gone against all your training, not to mention a direct order from your C.O."

Jack frowned and thought this over a while, picking his ear with his pinky. "You're right, and I can't even argue with you, Les. It all went down like you say."

"But . . . ?"

"But I can still hear his wife and kids cryin' over him, and beatin' me in the chest. That's why I preferred it back in artillery. My crew had over 240 kills, according to the F.O.'s [Forward Observers], and all of 'em put together didn't fuck me up like that one. Just seein' the faces of his kids, and to think what I took from them— how can I ever get over that?"

"Jack, look, of course it hurts, it's *supposed* to hurt, and the more you know about your enemy—the more real and human they are to you in death—the worse it's gonna be," said Lightfoot softly. "But let me ask you this, what if the old man had had no family, or if he'd been a kid your age, say, in black pajamas—would it have been any less painful to kill him, you think?"

Jack squints at her, suspecting a trap. "Well, yeah, probably, I guess. I mean, his mother and father would've missed him, I'm sure, but nobody was really *dependin'* on him."

"Oh no? How about the kids he'd never grow up to have? Imagine if *you* were the nineteen-year-old kid that got killed, and because of that, Alison and Nicky had never been born? Would that've been any less tragic than the old man?"

Jack grunted as if he'd just gotten a knee in the gut. Those two kids were the entire world to him, the only sweet spots in a life otherwise poisoned to its roots. His foul-mouthed mother had reviled him since infancy, and his father beat him up so often at bedtime that he cavalierly called the whippings "sleeping pills." No, nobody had ever loved him except his two children, and his gratitude to them was immense, inexpressible. "I—I see what you're sayin'," he murmured in a fog. "I never really thought of it like that. . . ."

Lightfoot let the silence do its work for a moment, then said, "Everyone who died there left something precious behind, and even the guys who came back from it lost something precious, too. It's called *war*, Jack, and it's time you let yourself off the hook for having fought it. Twenty-five years is more than enough time served—especially for a scared and mixed-up nineteen-year-old."

IT WILL BE ABUNDANTLY CLEAR BY NOW THAT Lightfoot is no shrinking violet in session. She can't afford to be: her clients have made a terrible mess of their lives, and need every bit of steering they can get from her. Jack, for instance, was flat-on-his-back broke when he began with her, and psychically incapable of even part-time work. Thanks to public housing, he and Nicky had a roof over their heads, but his unemployment money had run out and there was nothing left to feed them but the most meager pittance from welfare. For weeks, Lightfoot had been on him to go downstairs and see Tommy Crossman, who handled the disability claims in the shelter's Social Security office. But Jack, so humiliated already by the terms of his pitched descent, kept shrugging his shoulders and fending her off.

Disability was for "assholes and scam artists," he sniffed, not for someone like him who'd always worked three jobs, and cleared fifty grand per in a bad year.

"It's this deadly combination of pride and self-loathing, and a lot of these guys have it in spades," says Lightfoot. "I'd tell him, 'Jack, you're sick and you need some down-time to recover, and who's more entitled to collect now than you?' But he'd say, 'Screw that noise, I'm someone who works through his problems, and I'll work through this one, too'—which, underneath the bluster, probably means something more like, 'I'm stupid and no good and I don't deserve a dime, and don't you try to tell me any different.'"

If you're a disabled veteran, there are essentially three kinds of aid available to you: SSDI, or disability income, which is based largely on what you've paid out in Social Security taxes over the years, and is available mainly to vets with a substantial work history; SSI, or Supplemental Security Income, which is available to all vets, regardless of work history; and VA disability money, which is available to vets with combat-related illness and injuries.

It should surprise no one, however, that most Vietnam vets with PTSD have never received any of the above. Rootless and estranged by definition, only a fraction of them are even aware that these awards exist, and those who do know are so daunted by the application process that few of them see it through. Let us say, for instance, that against the bitter experience of your buddies, you decide to file a claim for PTSD with the VA. You will need, first of all, to find a lawyer who is prepared to devote hundreds, perhaps even thousands, of hours to your case for the princely sum of ten dollars. That is not a misprint; under a statute dating back to 1864—and which was designed even then to stifle veterans' claims—ten dollars is the most a lawyer can command from a client who is suing the federal government for war benefits.

Next, you must conduct a paper chase that goes back as far as the sixties, writing away for your medical records to every hospital and rehab center you ever did time in, regardless of what sort of shambles your memory is in after twenty years of street drugs and Thorazine. Then, there is the small matter of finding a psychiatrist to support your claim, someone with enough skill and savvy about the effects of that war to draw your story out of you and document it compellingly on paper.

There is a second way for vets to file a claim with the VA, but it isn't much more effective than the first. If you are a 'Nam vet with PTSD and are emotionally intact enough to investigate your rights, you will discover that there are benevolent organizations like the DAV (Disabled American Veterans) that handle claims like yours for no charge. The DAV's caseworkers are, by and large, veterans like yourself who are bound and determined to get justice for their brothers. Unfortunately, they are also overwhelmed and understaffed, and may be juggling as many as 400 claims at a time, each one of which requires hours or days of strict attention to be nudged along the track. Then, there is the unholy logjam at the VA to consider. According to a recent article in the *Boston Globe*, the VA's appeals boards are behind by almost a million cases, and the backlog grows substantially every year. The upshot is that, for all the devotion of his DAV caseworkers, Jack's claim, filed *twelve* years ago, had still not been ruled on and had long since lost all reality to him.

It was against this sense of vexed futility, then, that Lightfoot was pushing Jack. Nonetheless, she kept pushing, and one day he gave in, and went downstairs to see Tommy

Crossman. Now, Crossman is one of those characters you couldn't make up at gunpoint: a flamboyantly out-of-the-closet gay vet who staggered into the shelter in 1990 on a thirty-year bender of cheap vodka, and who has since become one of the most beloved and essential figures in this rabidly homophobic place. He has the fixed sympathy of a brood mother and the unfailing patience of a priest, neither of which qualities is in great supply here. Every day, he sits down with these tight, tremulous men, and leads them through the brambles of an inch-thick application.

"Of *course* they're terrified about doing this—they're suddenly being asked to remember everything that haunts them, and the only way they've survived is by forgetting it all," Crossman says. "And then, my God, the stories that come out of them. You think, 'Well, by now, I *have* to have heard it all,' but every week, someone comes in here and blows my mind—and *trust* me, I do know the truth from bullshit. I've got guys who've been hiding under a blanket in their mother's house, or who've had so much electroshock since the war that they can't remember five *minutes* ago, let alone five years. But one way or another, I get enough out of them to write a claim, even if it's just bits and pieces. The drunks I'm especially good at filling in the blanks with, having been in every drunk tank from here to Maine myself. If all they remember is the first syllable of the name, I go, 'Yep, been there, got it. Proceed.'"

Crossman is one of four full-time claims writers in the office, which has been, by any measure, a wildly successful feature of the shelter. Having discovered that there are huge holes in the safety net in this country, Smith and his staff lobbied federal officials to fund an on-site Social Security office. Late in 1992, a $250,000 grant came through, underwriting a seventeen-month, make-good project. In those seventeen months, Crossman's office wrote nearly 600 claims on behalf of men in the building. Of those, over half have been approved or are still pending, a rate 50 percent better than the industry standard. No less impressive, the average processing time, which can stretch into years in other places, has been cut down to 90 days here.

Indeed, such is the earned credibility of the program that Crossman can now earmark certain cases for fast-tracked benefits. This is what happened with Jack, whose disability revealed itself even to the most cursory glance. Crossman documented his story, brought in a psychiatrist to diagnose him, and had a supervisor from the state DDS (Disability Determination Services) authorize the finding. Six weeks later, Jack got a letter awarding him $1,100 a month and a retroactive check for $12,000. I bumped into him the day he got the news. He was walking around the shelter with a dazed, wonky grin, looking like he'd just been ravished by an angel.

"I—I can't believe it," he spluttered, "this's gotta be a mistake. Nothin' good *ever* happens to me."

It turned out that the award notice had been sitting on top of his refrigerator for a week, unopened. "Man, I got *stacks* of mail up there. I'm afraid to look at any of it. Nothin' never came before except bad news and my ex-wife's Visa bills."

I suggested that he take a cab home and open up the rest of it, pronto. "Obviously, your luck is changing, Jack. You might be the big Publishers' Clearinghouse winner."

"This is all 'cause of Leslie," he murmured, shaking his head. "She's the first woman in my life who didn't tell me what a piece of shit I was. My mother, my ex-wife, even my big sisters—'You suck, you're lazy, you're stupid, you're a drunk.' At fifteen, I hadda leave home and sleep in my friends' basements because I just couldn't take it no more. I was really startin' to believe it inside."

"Well, if nothing else, that letter means you'll never have to sleep in somebody else's basement again."

He thought this over a moment and brightened by a full magnitude; in the last thirty months, he'd laid down in a lot of bad places, usually panicked and alone and feverish from crack. In fact, almost a year to the day before, he'd been hiding out in an apartment in Brockton, setting fire to his discharge papers before sticking his head in the oven. "That's right, huh? I *don't* have ta worry about that no more," he grinned, marveling at the terms of his new fortune. And then, without a blink, the light went out of his face, and in a voice entirely devoid of irony, he muttered, "Man, how the fuck am I gonna *manage* this?"

BY NOON THE NEXT DAY, THE GOOD NEWS WAS practically killing Jack. Sure enough, in one of those unopened envelopes on top of his refrigerator was a letter from the VA notifying him that his claim had at long last been approved, and that a check was en route for $27,000 in back benefits. Furthermore, having been certified 100 percent disabled, he would immediately begin getting $2,200 a month to live on, the maximum payout for service-connected illness. Slumped on the couch in Lightfoot's office, his slack face the color of his Red Sox cap, Jack looked like someone who'd just had a stroke, or was expecting one any second now.

"You gotta help me, Les, I'm not ready for this. It was all I could handle just doin' the 'Nam stuff in here."

"Jack, I appreciate that this is a lot to suddenly deal with, and we'll spend as much time as you want on why it's freaking you out," she said, "but I want to make sure first that you know you're allowed to enjoy it a little. I'll bet your kid's out throwing a block party now."

"But that's *exactly* what I'm afraid of—someone findin' out about it and . . ."

"And what? Who're they going to report you to, Jack?" she grinned. "'Hello, officers, I'd like to report an act of justice at 17 Court Street.'"

Jack sat up and lit a cigarette off the one he'd been smoking, this last addiction doing stand-in for all the others he'd kicked. "That's why I've been keepin' such a low profile these last four months, not goin' out at night or lettin' anyone know where I live. I mean, I got Nicky with me now and that's all I ever wanted. I get so much joy outta just cookin' a meal for him, or watchin' him with all his friends over after school. If she finds out now how much money I got, and that Nicky's gettin' his own check from the VA to boot—"

"Who, your ex-wife?"

"Who the hell else?" he snapped. "I mean, the only reason she ever wanted custody of him in the first place was 'cause he was worth money to her in child support. I'm tellin' you right now, if she tries to take him back from me— if she goes into court playin' that heartbroken-mother rag—"

"All right, look, let's stop it right here, Jack. No one— and I repeat, no one—is going to take Nicky away from you," Lightfoot assured him. "You're a great father, and you've been doing a wonderful job with him. No judge on the planet is going to send him back to live with her."

"I don't think you understand, Les—every time I ever had anything in this world, someone came along and snatched it offa me," Jack growled, working himself into seismic anger. "I'm not gonna sit here and let it happen again, you hear me? I won't, because I can't; I can't go through that again. I'll *kill* that fuckin' bitch before I let her."

Her brow furrowing in alarm, Lightfoot looked at him appraisingly. Jack had a history of making threats against his ex-wife, though as far as I had been able to determine, all the violence went the other way. In horror stories told me by their 15-year-old, Nicky, and documented by court records several inches thick, Trudy had beaten both kids with whatever came to hand—curling irons, closet rods, frying pans, and fists. Such, moreover, was her humiliation of her kids in public that Nicky's buddies offered to break in in the middle of the night and split her skull open with a bat. Nor was she particularly more temperate with Jack, hurling knives and dishes and hot coffee at him, to say nothing of her ceaseless verbal abuse.

But as Lightfoot took a careful sounding of his rage, trying to determine whether he constituted a danger to his ex-wife, I found myself thinking of the sundry losses that had provoked him. Twenty-eight years ago, Jack had enlisted in the Corps as a kid in dire need of a little respect. No one had lifted a finger when he ran away from home, or checked in with any of his teachers when he dropped out of high school—but all of that would change, he dreamed, the day he came back a Marine, swaggering up the front steps in those insuperable dress blues. They couldn't *help* but be proud then, seeing the cluster of medals, and hearing about his bravery in the fields of Da Nang. Jack had cosseted that dream and kept it near him for two years, through the steambath sadism of Parris Island and Camp Lejeune, and his white-knuckled arrival under fire in 'Nam, seeing the double stack of silver caskets on either side of the runway. The dream had companioned him when his best buddy Diaz went down, and cooled him out when he picked up the helmet of a downed pilot and found the head of the poor man still inside it. The dream had even survived somehow the thuggery on the barrier island, when his faith in the root decency of his fellow Marines died in a ditch with all of that caterwauling livestock.

Indeed, where other guys were shipping home footlockers of dope, or filling up their seabags with black market bounty, all Jack contrived to bring out of there was his dream, a little care-worn and salty but intact. In fact, it had only been enhanced by what he saw in the pages of his hometown paper, which followed him around dutifully to wherever he was in-country. Right there, on the cover of the *Somerville News*, were pictures of his high school buddies coming home to a hero's pageant of hugs and roses. Jack thanked God for this weekly totem of small-town politics, so blissfully remote from what he saw on TV, and fell into rhapsodies about his own return, beginning with a jubilant reception at the airport. He'd lay there all night, ignoring the rats and the incoming, and envision the house on Bay State Avenue festooned with posters and bunting, and the pine trees tied off with yellow ribbon. He'd walk up those front steps, hand his medals to his father, and assume his rightful place as the family champion and favorite son.

But for all the broad hints in his calls and letters home, there was no one to meet him at the airport when he got back, nor did anyone bother answering the phone at the house. Devastated, he charged it off to some fuckup of his, and caught a cab in, half-convinced that a surprise party awaited him. Except for a sister upstairs, however, who was enraged at being awoken, Jack found the place empty and unadorned for him. On the table in the kitchen was a note from his mother, saying they'd all gone up to the cottage in the country and he could come on ahead if he wanted to, though there really wasn't any room for him.

"I was so crushed, I ran outta the house and got fucked-up drunk, and stayed that way for three days running," he'd told Lightfoot in a voice stopped up with tears. "Two extra tours, sending all my money home to them, and it didn't matter enough to even *fake* they were happy. Really, what was it for, all this pain and misery? What was the point of sacrificin' myself if no one cared? They never even mentioned it to me, let alone said, 'Thank you, Jack. Thanks for stayin' over there so your brother Frankie could take care a' his newborn. Thanks for takin' the hit for the good of the family.'"

Jack had suppressed that memory for twenty-three years, and wept and wept the day it came to him in session, the first breach in the dam of all his saved-up sadness. Listening to him grieve over it, I thought, no *wonder* he married the first girl he happened to get pregnant, though even Trudy's friends told Jack that she had set him up. But when you're as heartbroken and rootless as Jack was after the war, even bad company looks better than no company at all. And for the first couple of years, at least, they seemed to make the best of it. They moved into the bottom half of her parents' two-family, and Jack took a job at her father's meat-packing plant, where in short order he worked his way up to chief steward. But then he and her old man fell out over labor hassles, Trudy got pregnant again, tightening the screws on Jack financially, and soon enough, things between them were as mephitic and fractionized as anything in the 47th Parallel.

But however stacked the odds against him in that house, Jack couldn't have been a great joy to live with, either. Never more than a half-step ahead of the frenzy in his soul, he worked and drank himself into a mute stupor, collapsing into bed after a six-pack or two to get four hours of tormented sleep. He was rarely there at night to help Trudy out with the kids, and on weekends he plopped down in front of the tube, narcotized on beer and cathode rays. He'd made a couple of faint attempts to tell her about Vietnam, but when she gave out that the subject bored and annoyed her, he stopped confiding in her altogether. Aside from her tirades and his dull retorts, their conversation soon devolved into the grunts and sulks that are the discourse of all dead marriages.

Since this is one of perhaps three books this season *not* devoted to the question of why damaged people marry each other, I won't belabor the point here. Suffice it to say that behind a marriage like Jack and Trudy's lie two sets of busted assumptions. I can only speculate on hers, since she angrily declined to speak on record, but for Jack, the fervent hope was that he'd finally get some tending, a little nurture after twenty-five years of grief and tissue damage. Like a lot of 'Nam vets, though, he'd come home without a scratch on him, and must have looked for all the world to Trudy like someone who could take care of *her*. Here, after all, was this four-square Marine, with his jaunty blond buzz-cut and a set of shoulders you could land a Cessna on. How, at 19, was she supposed to intuit his suffering, particularly since he'd never so much as hinted at it during their courtship? To be sure, he boozed and smoked too much grass, but hell, this was 1970. Compared to a lot of other 'Nam vets you saw in Somerville, especially the ones hanging around Powderhouse Park, with their death-ray stares and two-dollar bags of Chinese heroin, Jack was the very picture of ruddy temperance.

Indeed, it's easy to imagine that one night their first summer together, Trudy stole a look at him and said to herself, with pride, "Man, if *that* war didn't hurt him, nothing can; I'll always be protected by him." Picture her disappointment, then, when she discovered that her protector was a basket case, a man who couldn't even carry his own load, let alone hers. How duped she must have felt, how punitive of his weakness, since clearly it didn't evoke a great passage of sympathy in her. In fact, two days after Jack opened his award letters from the VA, Trudy sued him for alimony and child support ("Don't ask how she knows about the money, she's a witch; she knows *everything* that goes on inside my head," he fumed.) He was particularly vexed by her plea for child support, since neither of the two children were living at home with her. "It's not even about the money; she just wants me dead, or in so much fuckin' pain I go and take myself out," he concluded. "I'm tellin' you, it won't end, man, she'll never stop doggin' me. She's gonna haunt me to the grave like that old farmer I shot."

Whatever its intent, the effect of her suit quickly told on Jack. He stopped sleeping and fell into a deep depression, going back on the medications he'd been weaned of by Lightfoot. Emboldened, Trudy took to calling his house at all hours, shouting threats and accusations into the phone. When Jack did nothing to stop this, the son, incensed, began torturing him as well, insulting him roundly in front of his friends and disobeying him at every chance. So far from his threats as the vengeful ex-husband, Jack just stood there and took it from all sides, transfixed like a condemned man by the clock on the wall.

Consistent with this tack of standstill masochism, Jack showed up for the hearing in probate court unrepresented by a lawyer. Luckily for him, his ex-wife hadn't hired one, either, and for five hours, they took turns with the probate officer, a glum, harried woman who looked as if she'd rather be strung from a yardarm than stuck between these two. On a bench down the hall from them, I marked their eloquent body language: Jack slumped over, fixing the floor with his watery stare; Trudy bolt upright, feet shoulder-width apart, glaring bullets by the thirty-round clip at him.

Finally, at twenty to five, they went before the judge. Jack, who was countersuing for child support, raised his hand to ask a question. The judge, glowering at her gold watch, told him to put his hand down. He began to blurt it out anyway; she told him to keep his mouth shut. The judge and the probate officer did all the talking. The case took six and a half minutes to hear. Cutting off the probate officer in mid-sentence, the judge snatched up her papers to go and announced that a ruling would be in the mail by Friday.

Jack stood there a full minute, his eyes puddling with hurt, looking like a grunt who'd been abandoned by his unit. "She just shot me down, she wouldn't even listen to me," he croaked, fumbling dazedly with the zipper of his coat. "All's she hadda hear was the words *'Nam vet*, and I was over and out."

"Jack, I know it looked bad, but let's not make assumptions. She could still come down on your side," said Lightfoot, who'd been waiting in the hallway since nine in the morning, hoping to testify for him. "I mean, she didn't let Trudy say anything, either."

"Don't matter, it's all done. I'm history," he mumbled. "Every cent I just got went flyin' out the window. I'm back in the shitter again."

"You want to go talk about it somewhere, or are you going to be all right till I see you tomorrow?"

Jack said nothing, sending a heartsick gaze down Cambridge Street. And then, balling his big fists and bashing them together at the heels, he cried, *"What do I have to do, goddamnit? What do I have to do to get myself heard?"*

*   *   *

TWO MONTHS LATER, I MET JACK FOR DINNER IN one of those breadbox-size joints in the Italian North End. It was the Saturday before Memorial Day, and Jack was marking it in due fashion, razing his hair back to its Parris Island buzz-cut, and putting on a SEMPER FI T-shirt. He had dropped twenty pounds again, and nearly broke one of my ribs in a bear hug before sweeping me up bodily into the place.

"It's funny how things turn out," he grinned, draping a napkin across his lap. "I'm payin' her a hundred bucks a week that she doesn't deserve, and I've never been happier in my entire life."

Seven weeks before, in one of those jaw-dropping upsets that so enliven modern law, Jack had been awarded full child support from Trudy, whose request for alimony was celeritously denied. Though the ruling was soon overturned by a second judge, its effect upon Jack was undiluted: Someone Out There had finally listened. In fact, as it occurred to him shortly thereafter, *a lot* of people had begun listening to him lately—the VA, the Social Security system, and a brilliant and steadfast therapist, upon whose good offices he could always rely. Suddenly, that woe-is-me rag didn't wash anymore, and it was time to acknowledge the truth of what Lightfoot had been telling him—that as long as you're breathing in and breathing out, even 'Nam vets get the gift of a second chance.

"I haven't figured out yet what I'm gonna do with the rest of my life," he said. "I keep thinkin' of what I gotta do, instead of what I *wanna* do, which drives Leslie up the fuckin' tree. She goes, 'You already *did* your duty, Jack; now, go do your dream,' which, for me, is kinda rough, since most of my dreams have Viet Cong in 'em."

His bolting laughter took both of us by surprise, the first such effusion I'd heard out of him. Embarrassed by its loudness, he looked timorously around the room, as though someone might make trouble for him with the manager. "But I'll tell you what, though, I haven't had a nightmare in weeks, and when a memory or something comes up, I can sit there and deal with it and not go shootin' off in a panic. Matter of fact, I've been listening to a lotta the old stuff from the sixties lately, Hendrix, Creedence Clearwater, tryin' to take myself back there, get a taste of who I was and what all happened to me then. Nicky's seen the changes and got real curious about the 'Nam, we talked about it for three hours straight the other day. Outta nowhere, he says to me, 'You know what, Pop? I'm proud of you, man—you're like a hero, or something.' 'Yeah,' I said, 'or something,' and left it at that. But, man, it sure felt good to hear him say that."

CHAPTER FOUR

HE WAS A BLACK PANTHER FROM THE AGE OF 16, shooting out streetlights in the riots of '67, and plotting to bomb the precinct house in Dudley Square, a buck-wild commando in the only war he wanted to fight. Had it not been for 'Nam, in fact, Ron would never have survived the sixties, going down, guns up, in a mad minute with the cops, or in a Soledad-style jailbreak from the maximum joint upstate. But one of his high school teachers put the law on him for draft evasion, and he enlisted two hours before the posse showed up, shoving his Marine Corps recruitment papers under the noses of the feds. "They went ahead and beat the hell out of me, anyway," he laughs. "Nothing personal, you understand; just trying to keep in practice for the next crazy nigger."

In the crackpot logic of that war and its times, then, it makes a certain kind of lovely, loopy sense that Ron's best buddy in the Corps was a redneck, a huge country kid from bumfuck Georgia who'd never met a black before in his life. "I mean, I seen y'all on TV and in books and stuff, but I don' know if that-all counts," Nash confessed to him their first day in boot camp. "Somehow, y'all look much bigger in the flesh."

In short order, Ron was smitten with Nash's sugar-cane innocence and his proclivity for saying the first thing that popped into his head. They talked after lights out about what little they had in common—a love of horses, and fly fishing, and World War II movies. But mostly, they colored in the vast gaps in one another's consciousness, Nash telling Ron what it was like to grow up happy, Ron telling Nash what he knew about women, which, even at 18, was plenty. Then, as now, he was preposterously handsome, with the smooth, brown beauty of the young Marvin Gaye, and arms and shoulders cut in proud, rococo swoops. He'd lettered in two sports at Brighton High and was cock of the walk in Franklin Park, where the girls cured him fast of his native shyness and his strict obedience to his mother. By the time he joined the Corps, in fact, he'd been living on his own for two years, and had the strut and precocity of a natural born leader. Straight off, he was put in charge of his platoon at Parris Island, carrying the guidon and calling cadence on those thirty-mile death marches.

Hand in glove, he and Nash made it all the way over to 'Nam together, and were even assigned to the same company in the Second Battalion, an occurrence so unusual as to seem like fate to them. It was a stiff jolt, then, when they got separated in Quang Tri, Ron heading out on a tank to Dong Ha, Nash choppering north to the hellfire of Con Thien. This was Tet of 1968, and everyone knew what a trash-pit Con Thien was, taking constant thunder from the DMZ and counting off the days till it was overrun by the NVA.

"Keep your ass down, and your flak jacket on," Ron grunted, trying to sound salty saying good-bye to his buddy. "I'll be up there in a week, ten days tops, so tell Charlie to kick his shit to the curb and crawl on back to mama-san. I'm 'bout ready to go home and get us *both* some pussy."

As it developed, his brave chatter would better have been addressed to himself. A day out of Quang Tri, his convoy walked into a mortar trap. A dozen grunts died, including everyone in the lead tank, which was reduced to black slag by a direct hit below the turret. Ron, running forward to haul a sniper to safety, was dropped twice by shrapnel from the hip on down, the worst of four wounds being the chunk beneath his spine. The thing was still burning up like jet fuel inside him when they got him back to Da Nang and discovered they couldn't remove it without crippling him. He lay there in agony for weeks on his right side, unable to roll over or zone out the pain until he broke into the meds room and helped himself to some morphine. It was deep into February before they finally discharged him, by which time he'd long since lost track of his buddy. He was only hoping for news of Nash when he landed at Con Thien and found everyone running around the LZ, screaming.

"What the hell happened?" he asked a corpsman going by.

"We got hit with eighty-ones, is what the fuck happened!" snarled the corpsman.

"Eighty-ones? Wait a second, aren't those *our* guns?"

"You're fuckin'-A they are, and they just killed five guys here. Including that poor bastard there who just came down to meet his buddy."

Ron looked over to where the kid was pointing and saw Nash lying facedown in the dirt. "He was all hopped up about seein' some dude named Ron," added the corpsman. "Said he really wanted to surprise him when he stepped off the bird."

Ron went over and knelt down beside Nash, shaking him gently to wake him up. "He looked so damn peaceful, like he was just catching a nap there—and then I saw the blood on the back of his neck," he recalls. "Evidently, the

shrapnel had caught him just beneath the helmet, and bur-
rowed its way up into the base of his skull. Two inches
higher, and his helmet would've stopped it. Two inches
lower, his flak jacket would've caught it. And if it hadn'ta
been for me, he wouldn'ta been there in the first place, and
would be off riding horses in Texas or someplace."

We are sitting in Ron's room at the Leominster
Homestead, Lightfoot's drug and alcohol rehab unit sixty
miles west of Boston. Ron has been here for almost three
months now, writing poems and pacing the halls, waiting
for the wheels of justice to turn. In ten days, he will go
before a judge in district court and plead guilty to two
counts of assault and battery against his wife. Depending, in
no particular order, on the following—the judge's disposi-
tion on domestic violence; his sophistication about the stress
disorders of combat veterans; and his mood and digestion
on the day of sentencing—Ron will either be sent to prison
for five years, or to a PTSD program in Maine for three
months. There is no middle option being considered.

"I got up to the top of the hill," he continues, "and somebody started telling me how excited Nash was, asking every
chopper that came in if I was on it. It was all he could talk
about, joining up with me again, and he'd hung around a
hot LZ just waiting to surprise me. He'd even opened up
my seabag and showed the guys my photo album, bragging
about all the women I supposedly had back home. . . .

"I just walked around in a daze after that, not thinking
anything, not hearing anything, just dry-eyed and dead-
feeling from my head on down. All of a sudden, something
really weird started happening. Tens of thousands of drag-
onflies raised up out of the ground, just surging straight up
into the air all around us—and *exploded*. Everyone was
freaking out, hearing this *whoosh!* and watching those wings

fall, all bright and translucent and nothing left of the head and body. It shut us all up, not that anyone was saying much anyway, and we just stood there staring at the air and the trees. After that, I don't remember anything else for days and days. It's all gone now, I can't get back there, like a two-week blackout, or something."

"Yes, but don't let it detract from the wonderful work you've done on Nash," Lightfoot says from her seat by the window. "When we first started out here, you couldn't go two minutes without breaking down about him. Now, when you tell the story, I still hear the sadness in you, but it's like a trickle instead of a tidal wave."

"That's true," Ron assents in his handsome voice, the kind you sometimes hear on late-night radio, all velvet and mahogany, with a Courvoisier back. It is the voice of a man who was meticulously raised, brought forth by a mother who never gave him an inch and whose fierce care is everywhere apparent. His white shirt and khakis are impeccably starched, his beard as well groomed as the greens at Pebble Beach. And though he has essentially been homeless for a year and a half and itinerant for more than twenty, every object in the room is in showcase condition, from his ceremonial swords in their black, lacquered sheaths to his archives of Vietnam. It is as though his life is a museum and he its manic curator, preserving everything to show the world what happened to him, and how, in spite of all of it, he endures.

"It's worth repeating again and again," says Lightfoot. "You do the grief work, the symptoms go away. Ron was telling me before how his nightmares are way down, and the flashbacks are pretty much gone altogether."

"Is that right?" I ask. "What kinds of nightmares were you having—about Nash, or the war in general?"

He pauses, looking down at his hands in his lap, which are clasped in fierce attention. "*All* of my dreams have Nash in them, regardless of how they start," he says. "I always end up on the same damn chopper, heading down into the clearing at Con Thien. I'm screaming, *'Don't land! Don't land!'* at the pilot, but he goes and lands anyway, and I jump out in the middle of all this chaos. Someone starts yelling, 'Incoming!' and I see Nash just standing there, waving at me with this goofy grin on his face. I yell, 'Nash, man, get down!' but he just goes on smiling, and then there's an explosion and he's laying there in the mud."

The tears come on slowly, like perspiration, and for a while he talks through them, unaware that he's even crying. "Sometimes, I wake up then, with him dead at my feet, and I'm running after the bastards that messed up and killed him. Sometimes, I get him to an evac, and he lives. But always, I'm screaming at him, 'Why did you do it, man! Why did you go down to the LZ to meet me?'"

The tears turn to sobs, and the sobs to moans. For several minutes, we sit by in mute distress as Ron bobs there at the bottom of his waterfall grief. "You said I was through with this!" he wails at Lightfoot. "You said I had worked it out!"

"I'm sorry," she murmurs penitently, kneading her palms. "Sometimes, I want so much for you to feel better, I get ahead of myself."

Her remorse, however mild, pricks his ears, rousing him out of his sorrow. If there is one thing I have seen in the 'Nam vets I've met here, it is this alertness to the inflection of pain. Suffering is their media, their narrative and trade. Inured to it in themselves, they are mortified by it in others, and mobilize like dog soldiers to stamp it out.

"I'm okay, Les, really, I can talk about it now. I just got surprised by it, is all."

"Are you sure?" she frets, glancing at her watch. "I don't want you going down there again, and have to leave you like that for the weekend."

"No, no, I'm fine," he grins, wiping his face bashfully. "Now, are *you* gonna be okay for the weekend?"

Everybody laughs, a goosey whistle by the graveyard. Taking advantage of it, I ask Ron about the poster on his door, an enlargement of a name rubbed off of the Wall: *THOMAS P. NASH.*

"It's brung me a lot of peace," he murmurs, gazing upon it. "For the longest time, I didn't know where my buddy was. Now, I do—he's right here with me, and I'm takin' good care of my buddy."

"THIS IS UNBELIEVABLE," SAID THE MAJOR, LOOKing out the front fire port. "This is the best goddamn fighting hole I've seen in-country."

He was standing in the gun bunker Ron had built in Con Thien, a marvel of dirt and monomania. It began at the trench line ten feet back, and descended, at a low crouch, to an eight-by-eight chamber. He had dug it so deep you had to climb up on ammo crates to fire out of the front or side ports, which were slits carved into the hill with such cunning you couldn't see them even if you were looking straight at them. For the roof, he alternated three layers of sandbags with three layers of corrugated steel, topping it out with six inches of dirt so as to be utterly indistinguishable from the ground. Once, coming back from patrol with his crew, he stomped around for half an hour looking for his hootch, until he realized he was standing on top of it.

Why would anyone put so much care and toil into an eight-by-eight hole in the ground? They weren't handing out medals for architecture, after all, or making sergeants out of corporals on the basis of better landscaping. Moreover, if an NVA rocket happened to land on top of you, it didn't matter *how* many bags you'd lined the roof with—you were still going home to Mama in a six-foot ashtray.

"Yeah, everybody always said that to me, but I didn't give a fuck; I was going to be *entrenched*, goddamnit," says Ron. "If you weren't at Con Thien, you can't understand how bad it was—it was worse than the Rockpile, or Khe Sanh. Three klicks from the Zee, from entire *divisions* of Charlie, and you could see it just drove him crazy to have us there. Bombing us all hours of the day and night, sending wave after wave of his best troops to get us—it was just a question of *when*, not if, we were gonna get overrun. That's why I decided to become an M-60 gunner, and humped that thirty-pound hog around on my back. If they were gonna come for us, I was gonna go out blazing—and believe me, I wasn't *about* to run out of ammo."

Indeed, he'd been stealing it by the crate load from supply and stringing together thousands of rounds in his bunker, a huge, brass, belt-delivered snake. He ran wires in the doorway for any would-be sappers, and drew a perimeter of blasting caps around his bed, lest someone steal in and slit his throat while he slept. Call his obsession what you will—a sensible response to present danger, or the cankered extrusion of his guilt for Nash—it probably saved his life in Vietnam, where he was wounded twice more in a span of three months, and sent home with a pair of Purple Hearts. But once back in The World, that rabid hunger for safety began to eat him alive by inches, and quickly fulfilled its mute predictions of doom.

"You know that dream where you're running for your life, and suddenly your feet are frozen in concrete?" he asks.

"To me, that was no dream, that was my *life*, or vice versa; I couldn't hardly tell anymore. I'd lay up all night, just watching and listening, staring out the window for shadows. Finally, around dawn or so, I'd drift off to sleep, and wake up, *standing*, in the middle of the bed, taking a piss on my wife, Felicia, or throwing her on the floor. That woman loved me so much, she'd waited the whole three years for me— and I ran her out of my life in sixteen months. It wasn't just the nightmares and our Bonnie-and-Clyde lifestyle, picking up and running anytime I caught a vibe. It was my constant trippin' on her, jumping down her throat for piddly shit, as if the roof was gonna blow if she didn't fry my eggs right. Here I was, this used-to-be bad-ass black radical, and suddenly I'm sweating just the tiniest details, nutting out from sunup to sundown."

"Which, I should point out, is extremely common among combat vets," says Lightfoot. "When you've been exposed like they were to constant trauma, where the tiniest fuckup really *did* cost lives, what you wind up with is a first-class compulsive disorder. That little voice in your unconscious keeps saying, 'If I can just do everything right, maybe it'll come out different this time; maybe my buddy'll live, and I won't be so lonely and broken-hearted.' When what usually happens, instead, is you drive everyone else away—the control freak with nobody left in your life to control."

So it went for Ron, who kept digging for cover, and wound up entombed in it, like Kafka's burrow. Because of his great beauty, there was always another woman, someone willing to take up residence in the bunker with him, convinced she could bring him out of it. On the road map of his twenty-year flight from himself, they pop up like placenames, mere destinations: Felicia, Boston, sixteen months; Patti, San Francisco, four years; Holly, Japan, five years.

And so on and so on, every mile accounted for, every lap of the journey plotted in a different woman's care.

"He was so damn fine, and so A-plus charming, that he never had to answer for nothing to no one—some woman always picked up the slack for him," says Felicia, reached by phone in South Carolina, where she resettled eight years ago with her three young daughters. Now a 40-year-old social worker who was recently widowed, she was 16 when she married Ron right out of the Marines, swept a mile off her feet by him, she says.

"Oh my God, was he sexy, and a truly good man on top of it, but at the same time, so wired and so scared," she recalls. "If I tell you we moved seven times in that little time together, I'd probably be forgetting three more. We lived out of an old VW, and slept on a beach chair till it caved in, and stole the bread out of bakery trucks to have something to eat—but I loved him so much, you know, and we were together, and that was all that really mattered to me. I didn't even half-mind the crazy stuff—the time a car backfired and he dove into the gutter, and got up all soakin' wet with snow and garbage, or those nights he woke me up at three in the morning, screaming, 'Get down, Get down!' in his sleep.

"The thing is, I *knew* he was sick and needed to get him some help, but everywhere we went, the doctors didn't do shit for him. They wouldn't even give him pills to help him get to sleep, which right there was half his problem, I thought. If he could've ever caught more than two hours of sleep a night, maybe, I don't know, it might've cooled out his mind some, and we'd have ridden out the worst of it together.

"What I *do* know is that I couldn't hang another minute with that temper a' his; it was like livin' next to a keg a' dynamite. He had so much rage in him, and any little thing'd set it off, and then he'd start in with all that scream-ing and cursin', and puttin' his hands in your face. I was shocked by it, really, because I knew he wasn't raised like that. If anything, that man was loved *too* much; his mother thought he was God's own image."

Actually, by his own account and those of his siblings, Ron's boyhood was a laborious one. The oldest of four kids, he was raised in modest comfort by his mother, a dress designer. On the strength of her ambition and twelve-hour workdays, she kept steadily moving her family up the lad-der, first to the mixed suburbs of Cambridge and Brookline, then to a large house in peaceful Allston. The proud, austere daughter of an Episcopalian minister, she was never less than stringent with her children. She was hardest of all on Ron, however, regardless of what Felicia says, loading him down with endless responsibilities for fear that she would lose him to the streets. From the fourth grade on, he was put in charge of all the housework and appointed the full-time keeper of his brother and two sisters. Too saddled to make friends, he sang in the choir in junior high school and attended two different churches on Sunday, principally because those were his only chances to be around girls. His first love, in fact, was a skinny soprano named Donna Gaines, who for all her Baptist coyness grew up to be the steam queen Donna Summer. No sooner had the two of them fallen in lust, though, than they were wrenched apart by their parents, forbidden to so much as speak to one another again, upon pain of biblical correction.

Against such ham-fisted constraints, of course, Ron was bound to rebel, and when he did, he didn't half-step around. He grew his 'fro out like Huey Newton and started hanging with the brothers at Grove Hall, talking about the advent of armed black struggle while digging on the fly blond hippies. So fixed was his mother's mark upon him, though, that even as a Black Panther he had a job at IHOP, mopping floors and flipping pancakes to bring home extra money. And when the inevitable came to pass and she kicked him out of the house, Ron found himself a room in a place around the corner, and kept a vigilant eye on his brother and sisters.

I bring up the business of his childhood because one piece of it is prominent thereafter: the guilt of the overburdened son, that sense of being responsible somehow for everyone around him. Back home in The World, this is not the worst of all traits, inspiring in one an empathy for the poor, and a blind loyalty to the Boston Red Sox. But in Vietnam, it often contrived to get you killed or came back to dog you for the rest of your days. Certainly, nothing has so oppressed Ron and kept him in exile as the memories of the men he could not save. Like the rest of his close possessions, they are with him always, never more than a moment's length from reach.

For most of her three months with Ron, Lightfoot has been chipping away at those memories, working to undo their septic power. One by one, she has picked them apart, beginning with the astonishing tragedy of Nash and moving on to the others: Gomez, the newlywed who'd cried on Ron's shoulder all the way over to 'Nam together, and who turned up dead, a bullet in his heart, four weeks later in Da Nang; the nameless kid Ron had carried in from a rocket attack, who died an hour afterward on the medic's table; and Tommy T., Ron's one steady friend on the planet, who hadn't been sober a day since Vietnam, and who blew his brains out with his service .45.

With the skill of a crack attorney, Lightfoot has reopened

Ron's case against himself, successfully setting aside each of the original verdicts. And every step of the way, she has duly pointed out to him how much he has already paid, both in terms of love lost and main chances missed. Gazing around the room one day at the effluence of his talents—the tiny, meticulous figures in silver, sitting upon a bureau he elegantly restored; the chapbooks filled with poems and calligraphy in his gorgeous Japanese script—Lightfoot remarks that he is one of those rare people on the planet who can do anything he wants; instead, he has allowed himself to do nothing at all. He was a brilliant jeweler, teaching himself the trade from scratch, and walked away from it without a thought one day. He was a successful model, running his own agency in Japan, until he got deported for selling hash. His three botched marriages, the baby son he cannot visit, the terrible loneliness he has carved out for himself—"why, for Christ's sake," says Lightfoot, "the jails are full of serial killers who've gotten off easier than you."

And yet, for all the power of her oratory, Ron goes on clinging to his guilt, convinced that some piece of it is irrevocably his. They work back through his memories, reviewing the two dozen firefights, and the fifty-odd other contacts with the ghost-shadow Cong. And then one day, Ron comes in with a dream that opens onto the memory of a battle. He has told this story before, but there is something new in it today, a recollection of a shooting he had previously suppressed.

"We were on a mine-sweeping detail on the road to Dong Ha, maybe a day or so out of Quang Tri. Suddenly, we saw a couple of ARVNs running toward us, dropping down half their gear as they came. Gunfire started busting, that *crack-crack!* of an AK, and all of us got on line, moving forward to the ville. There was a row of hootches on our right, and I went into the first one to search it out, and it was dark in there and I couldn't see for shit, and as I'm moving I heard a noise in the other room. I went in weapon-first, and saw a door pop open, a hatch in the ground that someone was coming out of . . ."

Ron breaks off, sobbing. "Man, it all happened so fast, I didn't have time to blink—I had squeezed off a clip before I even knew what the fuck I'd done . . . I went over to the hole, and there was a girl laying in it, and a woman underneath her with a little baby in her arms. None of 'em were moving, and I backed up and ran outta there, and followed the other guys up to the river . . ."

Lightfoot crosses her legs and waits for him to cry it out, then gently leads him back and through the scene. Were there shots coming at them as they entered the ville? Yes, they'd walked into a VC crossfire, from behind them and across the river. What time of day was it? Around noon, and wicked hot; coming in out of the glare, his eyes couldn't refocus, and everything went to black on him in the hootch. Had he been in much action before? No, as a matter of fact, this was his first firefight; he'd only been in-country for twenty days.

Before he sees where she is going with this, she has built a case: he was blameless, another scared-shit FNG firing his weapon out of reflex in the dark. He protests: Who the hell is *she* to decide who's innocent—*she* wouldn't know a fire-fight from a fire hydrant.

"Maybe not," she says coolly, "but I know what that war was like. I've had at least a hundred guys come in here and tell me the exact same story; they freaked and pulled the trigger, and someone died who maybe shouldn't have. That's what happens in a people's war, Ron—a lot of *people* die, not just grunts and slopes. Maybe, yeah, looking back on it, there were some things we could've done differently, like, for instance, actually *trained* you guys how to fight in the jungle, instead of teaching you out of some manual in a classroom in South Carolina. You can't take kids, march 'em around the flagpole for eight weeks, and expect 'em to act all cool and salty when you drop 'em down in the bush. It'll never happen, man, and you know it."

Ron shakes his head: he doesn't want to discuss it anymore. Tomorrow, or Friday, he will come back at her in force, trotting out the half-dozen things he should've done instead. And when in fact he does, she will calmly shoot holes in them, chewing up his resistance like he sometimes chewed up banana trees, letting off some steam with his sweet-shooting M-60. For now, however, he wants to go ahead and tell the rest of the story, because there is something else in it he just remembered, something he can't believe he ever forgot about in the first place.

"I had jumped into a hole and was firing at muzzle flashes across the river, when rounds started whizzing over our heads from somewhere behind us. We were all FNGs and no one was giving us any orders, so I yelled, 'Pull back!' to all the guys and started running toward the hootch. In the doorway, there was a GI crouched down, and I yelled, 'Pull back!' to him two or three times, but he didn't budge, so I just said, 'Fuck it,' and kept moving. Now mortar rounds started dropping and we hit the dirt, bunched up together like a gang of assholes. Up ahead on a dirt mound I saw this sniper of ours, shooting at the mortar tube with his spotter beside him. Right then, a shell came in real close by, missing me clean but wounding both of them. Out of instinct, I ran forward, yelling, 'You're gonna be all right, Marine!' and as I bent over to pick him up, I felt this thing like a lit cigar, burning me all up and down my ass and my legs. I was rolling around on the ground, trying to put the fire out, when someone scooped me up and ran with me over his shoulder. He didn't get but hardly three, four steps when another round came in, and threw us both face-first into a paddy. I was pinned down at the bottom of it with his dead weight on top of me, trying to push on up but there was nothing to push against but this slime, and I was sinking even deeper in it and panicking and starting to choke when someone pulled me up out of it and dragged me back to the convoy"—Ron sobs—"I don't even know how he saw me, man, I was two feet under and drowning, *gone*. . . . He saved my fucking life. . . ."

By now, he is trembling and hyperventilating, submerged in the viscid memory. "What are you feeling?" demands Lightfoot, planting herself in his sightline. "I want to know what it feels like, in words."

"I'm—I'm *scared*, man, I'm so fucked-up scared," he gasps, both feet going like jackhammers on the floor. "It's like it's happening to me all over again and I can't fuckin' breathe—my heart is like it's ready to explode—"

Lightfoot steps in and walks him through the worst of it, bringing him down slowly in deep, even breaths. When he is sufficiently restored to himself in the moment, she asks him who he'd been crying for, himself or the kid who'd died carrying him. "That's what I just now remembered, who he was," Ron murmurs, looking up with dolorous eyes. "It was that dude I had yelled at in the doorway of the hootch, telling him to pull on back with us. Man, he was a *first fucking lieutenant*, is who the hell he was, and here I am giving *him* orders. . . . In the hospital, they told me what his name and outfit was. I'd never even seen him before, but yet he ran out and got me, and wound up paying for it with his life. Why did he *do* that, Leslie? I wasn't shit to him, just another swinging dick in a steel pot. Why'd he have to go and do that for me?"

"For the same reason you had to go and risk your life for that sniper—because you were Marines, and Marines are trained to go back for their wounded," she says. "Do you remember his name now, or what unit he was with?"

"No, I don't," he groans, shaking his head mournfully. "Guy died saving my shit, and I can't even remember his name. That's pretty fucked-up, when you stop and think about it."

"Oh, Ron, stop it already—it's been twenty-six years," blurts Lightfoot. "The only thing that matters now is, is it important to find out who he was? Because that can be done—the Marines kept extremely accurate day records. If he was a first lieutenant, we can track down his name, if that's something you need to know."

"Yeah, it is," says Ron in a small, choked voice. "I need to go say something to him. I need to find him on the Wall and say, 'Thank you, Marine. Thank you for saving my life.'"

IT WOULD BE LOVELY, OF COURSE, TO LEAVE OFF here, to go out in a balm of lilacs and elegy and bid Ron Godspeed in his recovery. But this is not where it ends, as there is also the matter of Ron's violence, and the pass to which it has brought him. Because at some point, you discover that the world stops granting second chances, that for all your sense of righteous grievance, you are pretty well stuck with what you've got. Today, after two years of legal gridlock, Ron will stand up before that judge in Superior Court and find out whether he has one last second chance, or if, at the age of 46, he has finally used up his full complement.

As per usual in these matters, we show up to court at the appointed hour, and sit there in sweltering silence all day. While an elderly Brookline couple answer to multiple counts of child molestation, Ron fidgets in his seat and steals glances at his ex-wife. She is a small, delicate woman in a silk cream suit who at no time acknowledges his presence in court, not even when she stands up to ask the judge in a clear voice to please sentence her husband to the maximum allowable under law. It is a smashing display of fear and loathing, and yet, on three separate occasions, Ron leans over to ask if I too caught some sign or other of her ongoing love for him.

"Welcome to the land of total denial," grunts Lightfoot when I bring it up to her later. "The classic trademark of an abuser—'I don't beat my wife, I just *correct* her once in a while,' or '*I'm* not responsible for any of that stuff—the bitch brought it on herself.' Without a doubt, it's the hardest thing I do as a therapist, confronting them about their abuse without running them out of my office. But if I *don't* do it with them—and I've just started to now with Ron—all that other work'll just wind up out the window, because they're right back in court with the next woman they meet."

In so many ways, Ron's history with Lisa is typical of these kinds of affairs. When they met seven years ago through a mutual friend, she appeared as if by magic to combine everything he'd been looking for: a bright, intrepid spirit beneath her sweet-potato shyness, and a delicate, almost Oriental, pressed-paper beauty. Best of all, she seemed to understand him implicitly, to sense without being told that he was psychically wounded, and to love him the more generously for it. She brought him wonderful things to eat at work, gave him $100 books on Japanese art, and went canoeing and bike-riding and wandering with him, as much a kid sister as the great love of his life.

"Those first six months, she was like a gift from God to me, to make up for all the other shit I'd been put through since the 'Nam," Ron says. "But after sucking me in good and getting me real cozy with her—almost, you might even say, *addicted* to her—she turned right around and cold shut me down, flipping 180 degrees in a heartbeat. She would stop talking to me for days, without even telling me where I had messed up, and slowed the sex down to maybe once a month, which drove me out the fucking window. It was like, before I moved in with her, I was Mr. Right. One month later, I was Mr. Wrong, and no matter how many times I brought her flowers, or slipped a poem inside her lunch bag about how much I loved her, it seemed like nothing I could do would bring back that feeling. But yet I kept trying, right up to the time she had me arrested for—get this—sending her a card on Mother's Day."

It would be fascinating, of course, to hear Lisa's side of it, particularly about why she married Ron and had a child with him after what even *he* calls "five miserable, fucked-up years together." But so tenuous is his present legal status, and so broad the provisions of her restraining order against him, that his lawyer begged me not to approach her for an interview, lest it somehow be construed as a contact from Ron.

His version will have to serve, then, and it is hardly self-flattering. When they met in 1985, Ron had a small construction business that had kept him afloat for several years. But by the summer of 1987, when he moved in with her, the bottom had dropped out of the building market. They bickered endlessly about money and about his reluctance to switch careers, and when the tension between the two of them reached critical mass, Ron would shove her up against a wall or slap her hard in the face. Once, during a particularly vehement quarrel, he grabbed one of his swords and thrust the blade of it into their mattress, no farther than six inches from where she was sitting. Another time, he grabbed her by the throat with both hands, and though he swears he let go of her almost immediately, she fell down in a faint and didn't come to for several minutes. Ron was ultimately indicted for assault and battery, after a charge of attempted murder was thrown out.

"I get a little nervous talking about 'Nam vets and domestic violence, because it feeds into the idea that they're all savages and they're not," says Lightfoot during a break in our interminable day in court. "The fact is, some of the gentlest, most decent men I've ever known are Vietnam combat vets. But yes, a percentage of the men I treat, maybe even as many as half of them, have at some point abused their wives or girlfriends. Why do they do it? For the same reason *any* man abuses a woman—to keep his foot on her, plain and simple. These are men who've had so little control in their lives—and certainly none on the battlefield, where it cost them the most—that they'll fight like hell to keep the one thing they *do* control. A lot of them have already lost everything else—their friends, their families, their kids, their jobs, and they'd literally rather die than be left alone by her. She's their caretaker, their twenty-four-hour-a-day, unpaid nurse who's not even human to them until she decides to walk out—and then, look out below, because it's bombs away, folks. He'll do anything in his power to keep her in that house, including kill her or pound her within an inch of her life."

Lightfoot certainly knows whereof she speaks. Five years ago, her boyfriend, a 'Nam vet from whom she was separated, broke into her lakefront cottage and beat her into a near-coma on her living room floor. And even after he did time for it (a whopping *eighteen months* with parole), he continued to stalk Lightfoot and terrorize her at night until he died of an overdose in 1992.

But far from being run, screaming, out of the business, Lightfoot promptly adopted his three young children and redoubled her pledge to Vietnam vets. "This isn't to excuse what Michael did to me, because there *is* no excuse for battering a woman, I don't give a damn *how* sick you are. But even at the end, I couldn't dismiss him as a monster. Because, underneath the booze and the drugs and the symptoms, there was still a guy capable of being helped by someone," she says, walking back upstairs to courtroom 6B. "Maybe, yes, that's just my own guilt talking, but look at Jack twelve months ago, look at Ron *three* months ago—you know, for all their pain and suffering, these guys are pretty resilient characters. They made it out of the jungle at the age of eighteen, and at forty-something, after all these winters on the streets of *Boston*, for Christ's sake, they're still together enough to come ask for help. I mean, who the hell am I to say no to any of them?

"That's why, unless they've got a real history of violent crime, I'll go to court and ask the judge to consider treatment instead of jail time. Because let's face it, at their age now, if you send 'em away for five years, their lives are essentially over and done with. But send them to a program like the one in Maine, or remand them to the shelter for intensive therapy, and six months down the road, you've maybe got a different guy. Someone who's sober, and respectful of other people's rights, and best of all, productive, paying taxes *into* the system instead of sucking them out. I mean, forget the *moral* issue of imprisoning a sick vet; it costs forty grand a year to put 'em away, and who's got that kind of money to burn these days?"

*   *   *

A LITTLE BEFORE THREE O'CLOCK THAT AFTER-noon, Lightfoot is called into a conference in judge's chambers, with Ron's lawyer and the assistant D.A. They are gone almost an hour, and while Ron and I sit by, sore-assed and jittery, he mutters his hopes and plans to me like a juju incantation.

"First off, I'm gonna go back to probate court and file for my rights to see Kyle. Lisa hasn't let me see him in almost two years, since he was six months old. Then, I'm gonna go ahead and get my GED, and enroll somewhere close by, like Fitchburg State. And while I'm working on my bachelor's, I'll apply for a job at Leslie's place, training as an assistant counselor or what-have-you, anything to get my foot in the door. Thanks to Leslie, I've finally figured out what I want to do with my life. I want to be a couples' therapist for Vietnam vets. There's so few of 'em out there, and so many of my brothers are going to jail behind it, and I think I could help 'em, man. In fact, I *know* I can. I'd come strong from the heart, which is the only thing they respond to, that love you can only have if you've been in the shit with them. And I've *been* there, man, oh fuck have I been there, and right now I feel like I can't come *back* from there unless I bring some of my brothers home with me."

Finally, around four, Lightfoot emerges from chambers, trailing an almost imperceptible smile. Behind her is Andrea Resnick, Ron's tough, pretty lawyer, looking as though she just stepped out of a sweat lodge. "All right, we got you a deal, Ron, but, by God, you better live by it, or you're gonna do the full five years," she says. "That D.A. is dead set on you doing time, so just one dirty urine sample, or one phone call to your wife, and you're going straight to jail. Do not pass Go, do not collect your two hundred dollars."

The judge, a young man so devoid of color he looks like an exposed snapshot of himself, solemnly sets forth the terms of the deal. Ron's sentence of five years in prison will be stayed, pending successful completion of the PTSD program in Maine and three years of strict adherence to an aftercare plan with Lightfoot. He is to find a job, pass random twice-a-week drug tests, and check in daily with his parole officer by phone, all the while keeping a far distance from Lisa.

"Your therapist spoke very movingly to me inside about the suffering you've been through since Vietnam," says the judge, looking at Ron with evident interest. "I'm not indifferent to that suffering, although frankly I admit I didn't know a great deal about it before today. But I'm not indifferent, either, to the fears of your wife, who has a right and a need to go about her business in safety from you. I'm urging you, therefore, to make the most of this chance. Get all the help you need now to put that war behind you, and get on with the rest of your life. Because if you don't, I'll have you right back where you're standing now, and you'll find out how short-lived my sympathy can be."

In the hallway outside, Ron weeps and hugs Lightfoot, then in a rather more formal way bends to hug Resnick, who shepherded him, pro bono, through the year and a half's proceedings. "Well, Ron, you just lost your right to bitch about the system," says Resnick. "Because, frankly, with all the heat on about battered women these days, that judge could've fried you in oil there."

"That's right," chimes Lightfoot, "I've seen it happen for lesser charges. And I'll tell you something else, now that this is finally over—don't you for one minute think that you're out of the woods yet. That program in Togus is gonna be a tough sonovabitch, particularly for someone who hates taking orders as much as you do. No matter what happens there, or how bad the politics, if they say 'Jump!' to you, your only answer is, 'How high, sir?'"

"That's right," says Resnick. "I've lost too much sleep over this case. You're a big, handsome guy with a good head on your shoulders; from now on, there *are* no excuses. I know you'll go out and conquer the world—but if you screw up, don't bother calling me again, because I don't want to hear it."

From the promontory of his high cheekbones, Ron looks down upon the two women. Something crackles in his eyes—the briefest transit of bitter pride—and then he stoops, picks up his briefcase, and is out into the street, the haughty warrior at large between hell and peace.

CHAPTER FIVE

HE WAS A GUY ON THE 4:45 OUT OF NEW YORK, another middle-aged man in a dark blue suit swirling his Amtrak scotch in a cup. He'd looked across the aisle and seen me rereading *Dispatches*, marveling anew—and probably aloud—at Michael Herr's magic prose, and asked me why I was so interested in that old war. When I told him, he nodded and looked out his window for a while, then asked why nobody ever wrote about guys like him—the Vietnam vets who *didn't* crack up.

"I guess it's good you're writing about the ones with problems, and I'm glad there's someone out there taking care of those guys," he said, "but what about all the rest of us? What about the couple of million kids who just did their jobs over there, and came home and got married and raised a family and had a career? Who kept getting up day after day, like I did, and went forward, never backward, and paid our taxes and took our kids to the park to hit grounders to 'em on Saturday? Why doesn't *our* story ever get told, why is it always the ones in Grand Central with the sign around their neck that get all of the play from you people?"

By now, he'd slid over into the aisle seat, and his speech

had taken on the timbre of old grievance. "See, I have a real problem with this image of us as outcasts and criminals. A lot of us *did* have families to come home to, people who loved us and stood by us unconditionally because they knew we'd done the right thing. This isn't a pick-and-choose democracy, you can't just show up for the wars that you like. I fought with as much honor and pride in my unit as any of those kids in Desert Storm. The only difference is, they fought in a war the United States government wanted to *win*."

And was that, I asked, the story he wanted told about men like him?

No, he shook his head after thinking it over a moment, staring into the last of his scotch. "The story is *we* hurt, too," he said in a voice that suddenly splintered. "I have a lot of bad thoughts, a lot of things I don't want to remember but they keep coming back anyway, but what the hell am I supposed to do about it? Where the hell am I supposed to go now, with two mortgages to pay and another kid in college, and say, 'Here, take this off me for a couple of months, I'm gonna go collapse in the corner there.'"

With that, he grabbed his briefcase and headed in the direction of the bar car, from which he didn't emerge until we were almost to Providence.

I never saw that man again, but I think of him occasionally, particularly when I run into Chuck Stransky, the shelter's director of financial planning. Stransky is one of very few vets on staff here who came on as an employee, not a client. Ken Smith and Mark Helberg have a firm policy of hiring from within, but it is easy to see why they made an exception with Stransky. He'd lived a remarkable life, full of content and measure, and brought, besides a stack of credentials to the table, a powerful, almost rabid sense of mission with him. He was one of those 'Nam vets who'd done all right for himself, having come home, earned three degrees, and gone straight to work in his profession. Insofar as that profession was acting, however, his success was rather more high-flown than other people's. He'd started out in the bustling theater in Chicago, had a year-and-a-half run on Broadway in David Mamet's *Glengarry Glen Ross*, and had gone off to Hollywood in the mid-eighties to try to make the near leap to stardom.

"I had a fairly good stretch out there for six, seven years, though I didn't get quite the lift out of *Glengarry* that Joe Mantegna did," he says. "What came through were mostly sitcoms and TV movies, the grunt work of acting, but I made an honest living and got to ply my craft, which is all an actor asks for on this planet. But at some point, the calls stopped coming from casting directors, and then the earthquake hit last January, and suddenly a lot of those old rivets and screws started popping in my head."

Actually, as Stransky will tell you, none of those old rivets and screws were especially tight in the first place. Though he'd been clean and sober since 1985, his life was still something of a weed-grown wreck after twenty-odd years of hard drinking. There'd been two bruising divorces, long periods of estrangement from his children, and a two-year love affair that was just then falling apart. And though the death of his career was perhaps the worst blow of all, opening old head wounds of pride and identity, he wasted no time in lavish self-pity and went out and earned a license as a financial counselor. He quickly got good at it and built up a practice, but found this did little to stanch the psychic bleeding or to check a new and enveloping sense of doom.

"I'd never felt anything like it, not even that first year back from 'Nam, when it was all I could do to get out of bed in the morning," he says. "This was worse than a depression, it was like being stalked by something—I was literally walking around afraid for my life. I thought maybe it would begin to lift a little when I came to work at the shelter, but if anything, it just got more oppressive. From day one, I ran into a shit-storm with the guys here, who told me exactly where I could shove my financial planning. Apparently, nobody had ever come in here and tried to do this stuff before, set up some sort of budget for these wild, impulsive bastards. As time went by, they started figuring out that I wasn't out to steal their money, that if we took their pension check from the VA and put it into mutual funds instead of lottery tickets, they'd probably come out a little better in the end. But Christ, was it hell trying to sell this program to them—I thought I was going to be the first guy to get fragged around here."

Indeed, the day I met Stransky, he was walking the floor in a deep funk, his head screwed down so low on his shoulders it looked like it was trying to tunnel between them. "Six months ago, these sons-of-bitches were sleeping in a doorway; now, they're drawing a check all of a sudden, they wanna go lease a Camaro," he snorted. "I tell them, 'Hey, buddy, I've got five words for you—first and last month's rent.'"

We strolled the new barracks of the spiffy second floor, admiring the just-finished juice bar and the hospital-quality nurses' station, and the fifty-yard rows of handsome melamine beds and lockers. Despite the hassles of his job, Chuck was deeply moved by all he saw here, the constant, can-do progress of the place. "You don't know what this does for me, being a piece of something this powerful. The bond is so deep, it's like being back in Vinh Long, where the ties between the brothers were to the heart, man, to the bone.

I keep remembering those poor kids coming back destroyed from search-and-destroy ops, and without a word out of their mouths, I knew exactly what had happened. Eighteen years old, and they'd just greased a bunch of civilians, and you could see that, sooner or later, it was gonna take them down, too, whether by the inch or by the yard. Fuck, what do you say to a kid who's seen that? 'Don't worry, brother—the blood's on all our hands.'"

Without a beat, I asked him if he'd be in the book.

"Christ, I'd love to, man, but I've got no story. I wasn't a grunt, you know."

Well, grunt or not, I said, it certainly sounded like he had a story.

"What, how I dealt acid and hung out in opium dens?" He snickered. "How I ran around like Robin Williams teaching the hookers to speak English? I don't think so, ace. Why don't you find someone who actually did something over there?"

"THE HELL THAT'S ALL HE DID OVER THERE—THAT guy's as fried as anyone in here!" yawped Lightfoot when I mentioned him to her. "I run into this all the time with the non-grunts—'Well, I didn't pick up a rifle and kill anyone, so how could I be sick?' Hey, pal, you didn't *have* to kill anyone to have combat trauma. A lot of those so-called non-combatants died in rocket and artillery attacks, or got gunned down by snipers or blown up by hang mines.

"Secondly, these guys forget how they were trained as soldiers. At Fort Ord, the first thing they taught you was you no longer existed as a person, that from now on your only reality was as part of this thing called the *unit*. Whatever your unit did, it completely defined you, whether you were the grunt that pulled the trigger or just the kid who peeled the potatoes. And while you were walking around the base feeling guilty by association, the grunts were busting your balls for having *not* killed anyone, for living it up in some office somewhere while they went out and got their asses whacked. These poor guys were damned if they did and damned if they didn't—which I'm sure is why so many of them lie about what they did there. If you're going to be treated like a fiend and a murderer, you may as well bask in it a little."

Three weeks later, however, in Lightfoot's office, Chuck was doing anything but basking. "I'm sorry, Leslie, but I wasn't a combat vet," he shrugged. "I drove a jeep, I did guard duty, I was a chaplain's assistant—I never even fired a shot there. Yeah, sure, there was incoming every night in Vinh Long, and yeah, I was up there in the tower with my grenade launcher, watching sappers get chopped up as they tried to penetrate our wire—but does any of that make me more than a REMF [Rear-Echelon MotherFucker]? Maybe it does in *your* book, but it doesn't in mine."

"I see," nodded Lightfoot, in mock-solemn agreement. "So, as a REMF, you were basically exempt from VC mortars; they really only applied to combat soldiers."

"Well, no, obviously not, but—"

"And if Charlie broke through the wire, you were also exempt from being slaughtered, right? I mean, you'd just go up and show them your papers, and off you'd go on your way. I'll bet they'd even drive you to the airport, huh?"

"Look, all I'm saying is, compared to the guys I served with—those poor kids in the Cav who'd come into my bunker to get stoned 'cause they had so much fucking murder on their hands—compared to those guys, I have no right. I'm not entitled to any of this."

"Any of what?"

Chuck closed his eyes; he'd begun sweating profusely, and his right hand was rattling on the armrest. "Of *this*—the panic and—and the fucking adrenaline rushes, and the same screaming nightmare for five goddamn years. I've spent so much of my life since 'Nam hating myself for these symptoms. Who the fuck am *I* to feel this sick and this angry? *I* wasn't out there in the bush every day; *I* didn't slog around and lose my legs in a hang mine. I was just Papa-san, the hippy who got everybody stoned, and who took care of some of the kids who couldn't take it anymore. The ones who'd just butchered some old farmer in his paddy and come sobbing to me with the details, then went staggering over to the EM club to beat the shit out of one another. See, I couldn't kill anyone there but I could listen all right, and since nobody else would do it, there'd be a different kid every day, downloading his pile of shit onto me. *'Papa-san, I hadda waste this chu hoi; the C.O. said, take no prisoners,'* or *'Papa-san, the first sergeant had us blahblahblah.'* And I'd sit there and listen to it and try and comfort the kid, while all the while my mind is going bullshit with rage, and it's all I can do not to go kill that first sergeant. Because I *can* do that, I can *easily* kill that sergeant, and all those other shit-for-brains who were somehow responsible for the lives of men. But I *didn't* do that, I just smoked another bone, and dropped a couple of tabs of acid so I could keep the lid on my rage. And when I got home, all that rage just came flying out of me, and me and my buddies from 'Nam terrorized the whole town, going bar to bar and party to party, just *turning out* the joint."

"Whoa!" said Lightfoot, grinning in spite of herself. "Where did all of *that* come from?"

Chuck pressed his fingertips against the sides of his

skull, as if to keep it from flying apart. "All my life, I've done at least one thing I'm proud of, and that's protect people from bullies. At thirteen, I beat up the seventeen-year-old punks in high school who came around terrorizing my friends. And at home, it was my job to protect my brothers from my father, who was the biggest, most sadistic bully of them all. But when I came back from the 'Nam, I was as bad as my old man, a drunk, evil bastard who didn't even need an excuse. I don't remember most of it, because I was in a twelve-year blackout, but even when I'd cut back on the booze, people said my anger filled up the room, and you couldn't turn your back on it for a second. I *hated* being that guy, it isn't the least bit who I am, and it damn sure isn't the kid who went over to Vietnam."

"Tell me a little about what that kid was like," said Lightfoot.

Chuck kneaded the back of his scalp, trying to slow himself down, but his eyes had the bulge of someone speeding toward a cliff. "Well, he was an alcoholic already, and a pretty deeply depressed kid, but you know what—he was also a pretty honorable guy. He stood up for women, and went out of his way to make friends with blacks, in spite of having a father who was one of the great racists of our time. But above all, that kid was a pie-eyed patriot. As a boy, I could recite the Declaration of Independence verbatim. Abraham Lincoln was my hero, and I lived in America the Great, and it was gonna be a *privilege* to protect it with my life. Instead, what we did to that country—no, pardon me, what *I* did to it, because I gave myself freely to it, I *participated*—put the lie to everything I'd ever believed in. It made me out a criminal, a traitor to my own conscience, and I feel so fucking ripped off, so betrayed, so raped"—he is sobbing now—"I feel like my soul was taken away from me, and I can never go get it back again. I wanted so desperately to do a good thing, to cleanse myself of all my old man's filth, and instead, I helped turn that beautiful country into a whorehouse. I helped turn it into a dope den and a two-dollar brothel, into some lunar shithole with bomb holes for craters. I mean, we walked into this Shangri-la with wild orchids and pineapples and rivers so full of fish you could pull 'em out with your bare hands, and we dropped more bombs on it than we dropped in all of World War II. I mean, who the hell bombs a river, anyway? Nothing can hide in there; they've got no strategic value. All you're doing is depriving some farmer of the one resource that's keeping him alive. And *this* is how you help these people, *this* is how you win their hearts and minds? No, pal, I don't think so.

"And then I come back and I'm at this party with a bunch of people, and I start crying and thinking about all my buddies over there, and someone says, 'Oh hell, man, cool out already, at least it's over for you now,' and I realized, No, you fucking bastards, it'll *never* be over for me. Because one day, someone'll set off a cherry bomb outside my window, and before I know it, I'll be under a couch holding my nuts in both hands. Or I'll be in a video store in L.A. watching us bomb Iraq, and suddenly I'm back up in that tower in Vinh Long, watching the choppers buzz by to trap Charlie in the wire, and the Cobras are swarming after 'em with all their mini-guns blazing, and I'm crying and having the shakes so bad I think I'm having a breakdown. And I say to myself, 'You *bastards*, you came and got me again, didn't ya? No matter where I run to, you always manage to find me, and now I have nowhere to hide anymore, and it's all just incoming every night and every day now.'"

For some time, we sat there in bombed-out silence, letting the motes and echoes settle. Chuck's face, minutes before a mask of stiff cordiality, hung slack about the jowls now, as if his cheeks had caved in. And Lightfoot, whose manner is an unflappable calm, regarded him with a look of the most stricken sympathy, bearing him up with damp eyes.

"You *can* get your soul back," she finally murmured, leaning in close to be heard. "That part you think was taken isn't gone at all; it's just in hiding somewhere. There's a lot for us to do here, a lot of anger and grief and garbage to plow through, but that kid's still very much alive down there, and I want to help you find him."

"Yeah?" Chuck grunted, nodding his head, although from the glaze of his eyes, it wasn't clear he'd even heard her.

"Absolutely. I've got this hour open every week if you want it, and there's a heavy bag and a bat in there [pointing to the adjoining office, a converted sound room] if you want to do some anger work."

Chuck squinted at her through a fog, as if he'd just noticed she was in the room with him. "You know who I'm really mad at?" he said, sitting up. "You know who I could literally kill now if he were sitting in your chair? That pale gray pencil-neck Robert MacNamara. When I read *A Bright Shining Lie*, and he said in March of '66 he knew it was a hopeless situation, I threw that book across the room. You bastard! You cocksucker! That's the month I got my draft notice. And he says, 'Politically, we can't get out right now, we're just gonna have to suck it up for a while. Take a hit of twenty thousand dead a year.' *We!* Hey, fuckface, I didn't see *you* over there in a steel pot and flak jacket. Who the fuck is this *we*?"

*　　　*　　　*

CHUCK STRANSKY IS WHAT MIGHT BE CALLED A second-generation PTSD sufferer. His father, the only son of a Moravian police chief, ran off to fight the Nazis as a strapping 17-year-old. He saw action all over the continent, and was gravely wounded in the Battle of France, where virtually his entire battalion was massacred at the Maginot Line. Barely able to walk again after hip-and-spine surgery, he spent the rest of his life in excruciating agony, no small part of it psychological. At night, when he got good and tanked on cheap vodka, he'd belabor his kids with the same war stories over and over again, weeping anew at every telling. Nor was there much chance of ducking out of these; he was a slab-shouldered sadist who punished every infraction, even those he didn't see.

"My father believed that all children should be beaten regularly, whether they deserved it or not, because you had to have done *something* that day to earn a whipping," Stransky says. "As the oldest kid in the house, I caught the worst of it from him, and it would basically go on until his arms got tired. I'd drop a fork on the floor at dinner, or speak when I wasn't supposed to, and the next thing I knew, I'd be running for my life, with him in hot pursuit behind me. Instead of grabbing me by the collar, he'd knock me down with a shot to the skull and beat me with a closed fist until I cried or passed out. As early as the age of seven, I can remember going off to school in the morning and being unable to sit down in class for all the welts on my ass.

"Years and years later, I finally confronted him about why he'd done this to me. In his thick Czech accent, he grunted, 'Reverse psychology—I did it to make you stronger.' Yeah, it made me stronger, all right; it also made me a mean, self-hating son-of-a-bitch who passed the shit on to other people. And the beauty part is, he never let up on me, not even when I was going strong on Broadway and Hollywood. He'd call me sometimes at night after he'd seen me on *Newhart* or *Murphy Brown,* and say, 'You know, my friend, you are not a star, and you'll never be a star. You are a failure, an embarrassment to me.' Finally, one day, I told him, 'Listen to me and listen closely, you bastard, because I'm not going to repeat myself. You are never to call me again, do you hear? I will call you once a month and see how you're getting on. That is my duty as a son and I'll do it like clockwork, but not one drop more, you prick.' I thought that'd kill him, but it did nothing of the kind. He lasted four more years on sheer spite."

To hear Chuck tell it, everything about the old man was maniacal, besides his capacity for booze and cruelty. He spoke seven languages, put in seventy-hour work weeks, and bought and sold two flourishing businesses, despite starting out a cripple with ten bucks in his pocket. From him, Chuck imbibed a taste for hard work, and from his mother a torrid thirst for literature. At 9, he was reading Dumas and Sir Walter Scott; at 13, he'd roared through Shakespeare and was on to Marlowe and Cervantes. The only refuge in that house was the written word, and it was in this fair purlieu that his mind took up residence. In high school, his passion opened onto the stage, and by the time he got to college, it was all he lived for, morphing himself through the sorcery of language. He got a bachelor's degree in theater at Southern Illinois, took his master's at the distinguished conservatory of Brandeis, and was launched with some fanfare into the stratum of rep theater, doing the classics in Chicago and the Midwest.

But if Stransky, who looked like the young Robert Taylor, had the heft and trajectory of a rising star, he also had a lot of dead weight holding him down. Vietnam was never more than a car backfire away, and every night he woke up from the same asphyxiating nightmare. In it, a huge thug who was always faceless had him up against a wall and was choking the life out of him. Most of the time, he'd wake up in the arms of his wife, Patty, who had to wade through a flurry of kicks and punches to roust him out of the dream; other times, he'd come to underneath the bed, with his own hands around his throat and squeezing hard. It didn't seem to matter anymore how much booze he was knocking back, or how many hits he'd taken off the bong before passing out; after ten years of doping himself, he was becoming immune to it, and meanwhile, here came the past at a headlong hurtle.

"In her neverending struggle to keep me alive and in one piece, Patty had me on what we called the Marijuana Maintenance Program," he says. "The deal was, I could smoke as much weed as I wanted and have a couple of beers besides, but the hard stuff I had to avoid like the plague. And apparently, it worked for a while, because I can actually *remember* some of what went on then, particularly the three years at Brandeis. I generally made it to class all right, and was always on time for rehearsal, and got to pour off a lot of that rage and energy in one production after another.

"But when I left that structured environment and went to work in local theater, suddenly all bets with her were off. Not that I'd been any angel before then—I knocked Patty around pretty good when I was drunk, and cheated on her viciously with whoever my co-star was. But now, I had a lot of free time on my hands, and would have all my buddies over during the day while I minded our youngest kid, Daniel. Here's this three-year-old boy running around the house, unsupervised, while Daddy and his pals are getting

151

loaded in the living room. One day, I hear this horrible crash in the kitchen. I run in, and Daniel's sitting in the middle of a pile of glass, having busted all my wineglasses one by one in a circle. I managed to pull him out of there before he cut himself to shreds, but what haunts me to this day—even more than seeing him there in all that glass—is the thought that hit me when I walked through that door—'Christ, you little bastard, what am I gonna drink my wine out of now?'"

There are a number of such flashes that still murder his sleep, or that electrify him in passing with a bolt of pure shame. In one, he is chasing Patty from room to room after she chastised him for getting canned from a good teaching job. He has ahold of her by the throat and is hitting her with his free hand when their 4-year-old, Katie, walks in and sees them. "Stop it!" she cries, her face scrunched up in tears. "I want you two to stay together!"

"Booze, you know, is the great neutralizer of remorse," he says, smoking cigarette after cigarette on my balcony one night. "For fifteen years, I did horrible things, and never felt a twinge of regret. It was only when I got sober, and started to try and make amends, that the guilt came down by the brickload. I'd be driving in L.A. somewhere and suddenly remember Katie crying, or see the look of total hatred on Danny's face when Patty held him up in front of her so that I would stop hitting her. . . ."

He goes silent for some time, canting his head back against the bricks, watching the gauze of his gray smoke tumble over the rail into the heartbreaking blue of late evening. "I can't tell you the feeling, man, it comes on me like a seizure, my whole body just starts quaking and trembling. It's what Patty always said, I was a monster in human's clothing, and the only thing I can say to that now is, I was in one fuck of a lot of pain. Of course, in trying to kill that pain, I wound up causing a lot more of it, but believe me, that was never my intention. Everything I've done in my life, from the time I was five years old, was to try to help people get *out* of pain, whether it was my younger brothers at home or the guys now at the shelter. I'm just, I've seen too much suffering, man, and I've lost too much time to it. I wanna be on the side that says, *'No more.'"*

To that end, he is now putting in burnout days, going from eight in the morning till nine at night in a state of borderline delirium. Like a lot of the shelter's staff, he has the savior jones bad, and cannot find it within him to say no. There is always another guy to see, another dude with his whole life in a duffel bag and his mind still clambering out of the Dumpster. And as Chuck talks about these men, and what it takes to help them—a nose for their dumbshit lies and red herrings and forbearance for the inevitable stumble and backslide—I find myself thinking of all the ghosts on his line, the ones he would have saved if only he could. There were his three dear buddies, just back from the 'Nam in '69, who clung to one another for life and sanity when no one else would go near them. The "Wastrels and Varlets," they called themselves, and for a year and a half solid they raised hell together, trying to ride out the madness in their hearts. Ray White had it the worst, having lived through Khe Sanh and come home with a cluster of Purple Hearts, but neither Paul Foskett nor Randy Johnson, who'd won a Silver Star, were in much better psychic shape. They grew their hair out, fronted Charles Manson beards, and fell into bars like dead men walking, spooking everyone else out the door. By 1971, Randy had drunk himself into the grave; Ray died soon thereafter in a prison knife fight; and Paul was hacked to pieces by machete in Puerto Rico, after a piddling drug deal went bad.

"We were all on that ride together, and there was no getting off it—the only reason I'm alive now is someone *pulled* me off," Chuck says, referring to Patty, who, all of 17 at the time, loved him back to some fraction of himself. "Maybe it's just that I saw less shit than them there, or because I had some part of me that the war hadn't killed yet, but that still doesn't answer the basic question—how come I'm here, and they're not? They weren't born criminals or gung-ho killers; they were just kids who had the ultimate bad luck to turn eighteen in '67. I mean, is it all just arbitrary, or is there some method here, some way to tell the dead men from the ones who make it?

"See, I've wasted a lot of my life trying to figure these things out. Like, what the hell were we doing over there in the first place? Were we really trying to do this righteous thing, save a bunch of poor farmers from the clutches of communism, and maybe snatch some of their gold and plutonium while we were there? Or were we sent over by butchers to kill women and children because we had hundreds of thousands of kids out of work on the streets here, and they scared the crap out of the gray suits in the White House basement? I mean, I've read everything I can get my hands on about that war, and I still don't understand it. Will someone please tell me what was the fucking point?"

A COUPLE OF WEEKS LATER, I RUN INTO STRANsky in the hallway and find that, if anything, he's even more frenetic. No longer content to sit in his second-floor office and wait for clients to drop by, he's all over the building now foraging for new ones. In the cafeteria on the main deck, he introduces himself around to the dozen or so stragglers idling in the booths after lunch. Some seem genuinely pleased to meet him and come across with details of their day-to-day status—how many hours a week they're working, how much money they've managed to save, and when they hope to be out of the shelter and into a place of their own. With each of these men, Chuck sits down and works the numbers, roughing out a more tenable budget for each and scheduling them for private appointments.

Several of the other vets, however, brush off his inquiry to talk about more pressing concerns: a ravening urge to go out and have that first drink, or some thick, nameless panic that is about to jump the rails and run them, screaming, to the hospital. He pulls these men aside and huddles with them, pressing them to go see their PTSD therapist or to make the AA meeting upstairs.

"That's a lot of the reason I'm here twelve hours a day, even though, by title, I'm just the financial counselor," he says. "If they say, 'Well, I don't like going to [AA] meetings, they suck,' I tell 'em to keep on going until they don't suck. 'Yeah, but God, man, this thirst will *not* go away.' Well, of course not; it's the natural state of an alcoholic to get drunk and stay drunk, and it's a bloody fucking miracle each day we don't. Go read the [AA text], I tell them, or go down the hall and see one of the substance abuse counselors, but don't just sit there with your guts churning butter. Put that power of desperation to work for you."

"And how is it that these guys know to talk to you about booze?" I ask.

"Oh, please," he laughs. "Recovering drunks can spot each other a mile away. I've been at parties where a complete stranger came up to me and said, 'I've gotta go sit down and talk to you, man. It's fucked-up *big-time* tonight.'"

Finally, having walked the equivalent of five miles

together, Stransky and I go upstairs to his airless office. Though it is well after six and the rest of the day staff has cleared out, we are constantly interrupted by knocks on the door: guys barging in to ask where their checks are or how to open up a savings account without a single piece of ID.

"Jesus *Christ*," Stransky grunts, bouncing up finally to lock the door. "Either I gotta post a dog out there at five o'clock, or drag my ass out of here and get a fucking life."

He pulls a stack of forms from his desk and shows me what he does. "The first thing I go after is a guy's credit history. TRW's terrific, they send me a report in ten days; Trans-Union, on the other hand, treats us like stepchildren, it always takes weeks and months to hear back from them. Anyway, once I see what the guy owes out, I set up a payment plan with each of his creditors. And if, like a lot of these guys, he's stiffed everyone and his uncle, I set him up with our legal counsel to consider filing for bankruptcy.

"Next, I set up a budget for him, which I can really only enforce if we're his rep payee [the designated disburser of his Social Security benefits]. If he's living in-house, I give him fifty dollars a week to play with and bank the rest of it in a high-interest account. If he's out on his own, I pay his rent and utilities out of that, and hand him over a check each week for what he reasonably needs to live on. But always, I make sure he's banking at least ten percent of his income, so that at the age of sixty-five, he's sitting on some sort of cushion. Naturally, most of these guys go bullshit over that—they can't think twenty *minutes* from now, let alone twenty years. But I keep pounding it into them that they've gotta plan ahead, that if they blow whatever money they get from the VA now, they'll be beaucoup sorry in the years to come.

"And you know, when you get down to it, I think that's

all we're really selling here—reality. What's real and what's a pipe dream, brothers? Is it realistic to blame everything on the big, bad VA, or did *you* maybe have some part to play in this? Is it realistic to think you can move out of here with fifty bucks in your pocket, or should you maybe stick around till you've got three or four grand? And is it realistic, after maybe six months or a year of therapy here, to say you're one hundred percent recovered and never come around again? Or should you maybe keep stopping by a couple of times a week and stick with your combat support group and your one-on-one with Leslie? Life is short, brother, but that war is *lonnng*, and nobody's getting out of it with just a hug and a handshake."

A COUPLE OF MONTHS LATER, I TAKE A RIDE UP with Chuck to the house of a friend on a lake. It is August, and the woods are teeming with deer, and pheasants trudge across the sloping lawn like old women in orthotic shoes. Chuck puts his feet up on the rail of the deck, takes a long, deep draft of the silver air, and says, "Man, it sure beats dying in a ditch, doesn't it?"

He looks about five years younger than the last time I saw him and has kicked, cold-turkey, his two-pack-a-day habit. "I just figured, hell, if the war and the booze didn't kill me, why give R. J. Reynolds the shot?" he shrugs. "Besides, things have calmed down a lot for me lately. I stopped doing those lunatic, twelve-hour days and am actually getting home now with enough energy to make dinner. It took me five months to find out that that place can become an addiction, and that you can't help anybody else if you're more fried than they are."

With his evenings and weekends free, he's begun to

teach acting part-time, and with a couple of buddies from 'Nam is trying to put together an evening of theater about the course of their lives since the war.

"Isn't it crazy? In 'Nam, all I wanted was to be a civilian, to get away from all that murder and corruption. But back home, I had so much rage, I couldn't *stand* being around civilians, and could only tolerate the company of other 'Nam vets. Now, after all these years of impersonating a civilian, I'm back here among the brothers again. But this time, it's different, it's about connecting, not hiding out. Wherever I wind up ten years from now, part of me is always gonna need to check back here with them, because in some way, they're my real family. I grew up with these guys, we came of age together, even if we weren't in-country at the same time. When I went over to 'Nam, I was just a kid, a baby. But a year later, when I came home, I was a very old man, and only these guys know what that felt like.

"But getting back to teaching, I'd forgotten what a blast it is. All that adrenaline they bring, that pure hunger to learn. It takes me back to 'Nam, where I taught in a Quaker school in Can Tho. Can you picture it, man? The Cav's coming back from a firefight with Charlie, and I'm walking by them to teach English to Charlie's sisters. The C.O. hated me for it, kept calling me a fag and a commie sympathizer, but I told him I was nothing of the kind. I said, 'I came here to help, sir, and that's exactly what I'm doing. I mean, that *is* why we're over here, isn't it?'"

Chapter Six

ASK VIETNAM VETS WHICH MOVIES THEY LIKED about that war, and most of them tick off scenes, not titles. "Man, that Air Cav raid in *Apocalypse Now* was *live* like a bastard," or, "The first half-hour of *Full Metal Jacket* had me trippin' for two whole days." Ask them which character spoke to them the most, though, and almost all of them agree it was Sergeant Barnes in *Platoon*, the ice-in-the-veins jungle killer played by Tom Berenger. "Yo, that was *my* top sergeant through and through," they say. "The flak jacket open, no helmet on his head, just struttin' through the bush like, 'Don't even *dream* it, motherfuckers.'"

Although there is no physical resemblance to speak of, I thought of Sergeant Barnes when I first met Jim F. at the shelter. For one thing, Jim *loved* his tour in Vietnam, mowing down the country in his fifty-ton tank and burying Charlie by the battalion in the Iron Triangle. For another, the darkness seeps out of him from every pore, enveloping you instantly in its sooty murk.

"Shit, if anything, I *miss* that war; my only regret is I didn't re-up," he snorts. "'Course, if the bastards hadn'ta tied our hands behind our backs, telling us to brake for women and children, we'd've torched the whole country and killed 'em all and been back home in time for Christmas."

He is a huge, blond man with fists the size of mush melons and circles under his eyes that look like they've been applied with lamp-black. Among Vietnam vets, his is a common-enough complaint, that only the cowards in Washington, with all their balky rules of engagement, prevented them from winning the war in a walk-over. But from Jim, it is less a lament than a jeremiad, the extrusion of twenty-five years of bile.

"The VC were warriors, don't get me wrong now, the baddest little fuckers this country ever fought, but they had no answer for American tanks," he bristles. "For example, the Ninth Division of the Viet Cong had been dug into the Iron Triangle since sometime back in the early fifties, and fortified it so thick they flew their flags from the village gates—and in less than two months, we totally *annihilated* 'em. They tried to stand and fight, but it was a fuckin' joke, a slaughter. What the fuck were they gonna do against maximum armor? We [the 11th Armored Cavalry, the fabled Blackhorse Regiment] came at 'em with tanks, gunships, APCs, Phantoms, slicks, Puff the Magic Dragon—nothin' on the fuckin' planet could've held us back. And we didn't just oust 'em, we burnt their shit to the ground, huge villages that had been there for five thousand years. We blew up factories and ammo dumps and underground hospitals, bunkers that had been hardened with slabs of concrete. We brought in Chinooks and got rid of ten thousand people, sent every old man, woman, child, and animal to refugee camps on the coast. And what do you think happened after we completed our mission, and rolled it all over as flat as daylight? Fucking MACV ordered us down to Long Binh, and in less than four weeks, the Cong were back in the Triangle again, makin' themselves at home like they'd just stepped out for a fuckin' smoke."

He laughs his great, black, gurgling laugh, and straight-away you see him in the hatch of that tank, doing thunder runs with the top down and his head up high, insensible against fear and pity. Unlike most tank commanders, Jim rarely wore a helmet, and couldn't bear coming down off the jump seat he stood on, though it made him a fat target for roadside snipers.

"Ah, that never bothered me, I thought I was invulnerable," he shrugs. "We got mined every day and mortared every night, six or eight rounds to let us know they were out there. But I truly believed that nothing could stop us, that if they got off our fuckin' backs and let us fight like warriors, we [the Cav] could win the war single-handed. But it was, 'No, don't shoot *those* gooks, they're civilians,' and 'Don't touch *that* ville, Captain's orders,' so by the time they came to me in February and said, 'You, you're outta here,' I hopped up on that laundry truck and didn't even look back. I mean, yeah, I loved my crew and I loved my tank, but how can you go on fighting like that? The way I look at it, there's only one rule in war, and that is, *There are no rules.*"

As if to illustrate this, he tells you about that morning in Xuy Kat, when he jumped off his tank, popped a can of beans and meatballs, and sat down to eat on a pile of fresh corpses. There were 109 enemy dead stacked up, dragged in from the bush after an ambush gone wrong, and here and there stray arms and legs from the maimed who'd managed to crawl off, swathing the bush with their blood trails.

"In thirty-six hours, we wiped out two battalions, the 272nd and 273rd VC," he boasts. "For the second time in a week, they'd tried to jump one of our convoys, and both times it happened, we were just down the road from them. Ten minutes flat, we were rolling through the kill zone, wasting everything around in a three-hundred-yard arc. We hit 'em with H/E and white phosphorous and 90-mm shells, and cannister rounds that came out of the tube like buckshot, spraying the whole area with long, flat pellets that tore you up for days. Fact is, we'd probably whacked most of 'em out that first night, but we were so jacked up on speed and combat juice that we kept firing for another whole day.

"Finally, the morning of December fifth, we went out and gathered up all the bodies, and brought 'em on back to the road. No sooner had we finished stacking them than I heard my stomach growling, like, 'Yo, I wonder what these crispy critters taste like?' I thought, *Christ, fuck me, am I that far gone?* when I heard the stomachs of the other guys growling, too. Then it hit me—we hadn't eaten in two days, so I told 'em to fall out and grab some breakfast, and we plopped down on those corpses and ate our C-rats, and mugged with the bodies for snapshots.

"Next thing I know, the captain comes up to me and says, 'Yo, you see all them vultures over that area? I think there's bodies in there; go get 'em.' At this point, I'm so wrecked and godlike from killing that I don't even take backup with me, just go following out the elephant grass to where the buzzards are circling. As I stepped into the clearing, I saw a gook by a tree, propped up against it holding his intestines in his hand. He'd obviously been sitting there, dying, the whole night, but he had enough strength left to hold up his AK with the other arm. It was pointed at my chest and he could've easily squeezed one off on me, but his eyes locked on to mine and said, 'Leave me alone, man.

I'm dying, and I don't wanna do this anymore. If you go back the way you came, I won't zap you out; just split, and let me go to my god in peace.' I stepped back *realll* slowly, never raising my grease gun, and turned and walked out of there without saying a word. He had the drop on me and could've done me and not even blinked, but he didn't and I'll never forget that as long as I live. That's one reason I have so much respect for Charlie. He might've been small and underfed and even younger than we were, but, motherfucker, he had balls and heart. I'd have felt no shame in losing to an opponent like that—except that, like I say, he didn't beat us—we did."

BY THE END OF THE DAY, YOU'VE HEARD ENOUGH of these stories to think, aha, so *that's* his illness. Not the usual infection of guilt, grief, and rage, but a morbidity that dials down the blood in his heart to a coldness approaching absolute zero. Nowhere to be seen in him are uncried tears or trace elements of anguish or vitrified self-pity. "I am what that war made me," Jim says with a shrug. "Vietnam was the best dope I ever smoked, the best whore I ever fucked. She stole my fucking soul, and I was happy to let her have it."

But then the next day, he shows up with a leather portfolio containing slides of some of the most extraordinary artwork: a pen-and-ink self-portrait that reminds you a good deal of the later Dürer; a charcoal nude that won him the First Prize for drawing at the salons of Baden-Baden and the Palais de Luxembourg; and an assortment of paintings that in scale and color seem equal parts Bosch and Rothko. And you find out that, far from running around enacting his rage, Jim has for the better part of the past twenty-five years been almost wholly engaged in making and teaching art. He holds two degrees in painting, including a master's from Boston University, has taught with distinction at a number of places, and was for several years the chief executive of the Army's art programs in Europe, where he oversaw a staff of more than three hundred.

Indeed, until Desert Storm broke out in 1991 and swallowed up the budget for his $20-million-a-year operation, Jim's career track had taken him straight through the ceiling. Nine years earlier, he'd parlayed a job in a public high school into the directorship of the arts program at Fort Devens, Massachusetts. Such was the skill and élan with which he ran it that every couple of years, he got a quantum promotion, first to Nuremburg, then Berlin, where he was the Commandant's representative at cultural affairs of state.

"It was a great, beautiful ride, and I loved every minute of it," he says, the first strain of loss inching into his voice. "You know, there's a whole other side of me—the good angel, I call him—that comes out whenever I'm doing my work. Art is the one thing that's left from the kid that I was before I went over to Vietnam. When I came home in '67, I had no memories of that kid, I couldn't even pick him out in the family album. I'd just look at him in those pictures and say, 'Man, what the fuck were *you* smiling about?' That whole part of me was dead and buried.

"But even in 'Nam, when my bad angel was getting his rocks off, grooving on all that murder and mayhem, some part of me knew to look out for my good angel. Riding down the road in that M48 Patton, I always kept my right hand under the hatch, 'cause that was the hand that I drew and painted with. I was like, 'Go on, take my left hand, take the whole goddamn arm off, but leave my right one alone, because if I ever walk out of this stinking hole, I'm gonna need something to live for.' And I tell you straight up now, art's the only reason I'm still breathing, where so many of my buddies have checked out."

We talk a while longer about his drawings and paintings, and about the state he enters into when he is fast at work on them, going for whole days in a fever of adrenaline without stopping to eat or sleep. By degrees, I notice that the hardness has dropped out of him and a passage of tenderness opened up. Where before he cursed constantly, fairly oozing invective, now he speaks softly in the flush, ardent cadence of a man possessed by his craft. It is the voice not of some disembodied aspect of character but of true self stepping out from behind the plate armor to declare itself in all its complexity.

"Before, when I told you I felt nothing when I left 'Nam—that isn't exactly how it went down," he says. "I mean, yeah, I was numb when I got on the plane, but I'd just been stalking the Cong for two weeks, closing up the circle on him in [Operation] Junction City. Also, when I looked across the floor of the C-140, there were fifty silver caskets going home for burial. That froze me down solid until I got in the car with my wife, and then she started in about the brakes on the car, and the new stove she'd just bought that wasn't heating properly, and suddenly I got hit with this humongous guilt wave—you mean I left my buddies behind in Xuan Loc for *this*? We were tighter than just a tank crew, we were like family, a *real* one, and I left them just standing there, looking at me in shock. A couple of months later, I got a letter from one of them in the hospital, telling me they'd gotten blown up running over a booby-trapped plane bomb. I felt so much blame, I couldn't even write back to him, and I've been looking for the three of them everywhere since. I've tried writing to their parents, I've called directories all over the country—the only thing I haven't done is check for them on the Wall, because, man, if they're up there, it'll cut my heart up. As it is, I'm in jail still and only they can let me out, by showing up and telling me that I didn't betray them."

He goes on to describe how, in a stupor of guilt, he'd stumbled around for three years after the war, unable to restart his life. He'd come home from Vietnam with a case of month-old malaria and was so sick and exhausted he could barely stagger to the bathroom. Nevertheless, that first Sunday, his mother-in-law came downstairs for breakfast and threw the *Globe* want ads across the table at him. "Nobody sits around on their ass being taken care of here," she said. "Go out and get a job if you're gonna live in this house."

"It was totally surreal, unbelievable; I really thought I'd landed on Mars," he mutters. "Six months straight of triple-canopy jungle, no downtime, no slack, just murder and more murder—and these two act like I'm just back from the candy store. No compassion about what I'd been through, not even idle curiosity; when I'd try to bring up the war, they'd just shoot me down with these looks like, Who the hell *cares*, already?

"And then I dragged myself over to the VA in Manchester, and they said, '*Malaria?* Get lost, son, we don't treat that in New Hampshire. You want help for tropical diseases, try the VA in Puerto Rico.' In fact, if it hadn't've been for this friend of my mother-in-law's, an old WW II vet from the South Pacific who for some reason had hung on to his anti-malaria kit, I'd've wound up in a city hospital, laying in a pool of my own vomit for a month.

"But let me just say this in defense of the Manchester VA—this was February of '67, and I'm quite sure I was the first guy to walk in there from out of the bush. If it'd been six months, a year later, they'd have probably known what to do with me, but at that point, I must've looked like the Wild Man of Borneo to them."

As you soon come to see, this is a thing he does often, laying charges, then abruptly letting off the offender. About the shocking indifference of his first wife and mother-in-law, for instance, he says that like most Americans in 1967, they were utterly innocent about the war, thinking of it (to the extent that they could be said to have thought of it at all) as some trivial police action that would be over in a couple of months.

"They didn't get it then that there was a war going on because it didn't feel like one to them," he says. "No one was making sacrifices like my mom and I had done when my old man went to fight the Nazis under Patton." [Jim was born in 1938; he was 28 when he landed in Vietnam.] "They weren't going through gas rations or working around the clock in some shitty bomb factory; they were living their idiot little lives unchanged. I mean, when I got offa that plane and we were driving up to her mother's place, my wife actually said to me, 'Oh, honey, while you were away, they built a new mall in Manchester. I just want to swing by there and show it off to you.' Does that *sound* like someone with even half a clue?"

However gracious this is, it is also, of course, preposterous. Anyone who took one look at him that night would have known what it was he was coming back from. But in Jim's eyes, so base was his "betrayal" of his tank crew that it effectively cancels out all crimes against him. How, he asks, could he blame his wife for turning her back on him when he did the same thing to his brothers under fire? Moreover, as he later admits, if he'd allowed even a little of his hurt and rage to seep through, he'd have "snapped her neck for her while she was sitting there, and smoked a cigarette while [he] was waiting for the cops to come."

Instead, he withdrew both literally and figuratively into a bunker and never came out again as far as his wife was concerned. He got a job as a bellicose bill collector, bought a house with a VA loan in Hull, and installed himself for good in its three-quarters basement, keeping a constant vigil out the casement windows. At night, when his paranoia hit the ceiling, he'd low-crawl into the yard and hide behind the grape arbor, a one-man listening post on detail till dawn. He found it unbearable to be among crowds, couldn't get on the subway unless it was at least half-empty, and would only sit down in a bar or diner if he could have his back to the corner. And on the rare occasions he allowed his wife to drag him to parties, he'd scare the living daylights out of her hoity-toity friends with a leering impersonation of himself.

"Without fail," he sniggers, "one of them would get a few belts inside of them and come up to me and say, 'I understand you fought in the war in Vietnam. Did you ever actually . . . kill anyone there?' 'Oh yes, my dear,' I'd say in this horror-movie voice, 'and nothing but women and children, too. Do you want to know what they *smelled* like?'"

For the sake of their two kids, Jim and his wife stayed married for twenty years, though you'd have needed a hammer and chisel, he says, to chip the ice between them. In 1970, he quit his job abruptly and went to college on the GI Bill, where, in his camouflage jacket and jungle boots, he ran into a lot of other 'Nam vets. Discovering they were all afflicted with a multitude of the same things, they formed a political action group and joined the coalition that was emerging at other colleges in the state. Like a lot of his new buddies, Jim was suffering from a recurrent illness that none of the doctors could diagnose. A high fever would set in, accompanied by chest and joint pains that would lay him up for a month. Whenever he went to the beach with his kids or was otherwise exposed to the sun, his skin would fall off him in lengthwise folds, literally unraveling like a snake's.

"That had me freaked out, but what happened to my family was worse," he says. "My wife, who had a healthy baby before I went to 'Nam, had six spontaneous miscarriages after I came back, and had to have a radical hysterectomy at the age of twenty-six. What's more, our second child was born with a weird deformity and these terrible, unexplained fevers, where they had to plunge him in ice all the time just to keep him alive. He's a big, handsome guy now, doing brilliantly in college, but as a kid, he had all kinds of learning disabilities—dyslexia, hyperactivity, attention-deficit disorder—and so many of my buddies' kids had the exact same symptoms. And then there were the ones with even *worse*—Jim Crabtree's daughter, who was born with no vagina and no rectum, they had to be created in the hospital; another guy, his kid came out with no eyes, just a sheath of skin where there should've been sockets. And believe me, I could go on, kids born without a *brain*, and all of us with babies like that felt so much guilt and agony. And not just about our kids but about our *kids'* kids as well—the doctors told us that the mutation I passed on to my son could easily be passed on to them, and more severely. That tears at my gut, man, I poisoned my whole family, and how do you just go up to 'em and say, 'I'm sorry about that?'

"One of the things I did when I first got involved in veteran activism was to join the Massachusetts chapter of Agent Orange Victims International. In fact, I was one of the fifty named plaintiffs who put up money for the suit against Dow Chemical, which eventually got settled out of court for millions. I mean, I was *there*, man, when they built the base camp at Long Binh, and the bastards went in and laid down so much dioxin, they turned deep jungle into a bald hill overnight. And we weren't just breathing it or walking around in it—we had to *bed down* on that shit night after night. Whereas everybody else had hootches and bunkers, we [the Cav] were split out there on the perimeter, living in the dirt like a bunch of animals. No latrines, no running water—I think I took three showers in six months there, and when I came home and got in the shower, all this red stuff started pouring out of me. At first, I thought it was blood, you know, but there was just too much of it coming out of me, and it kept coming out and coming out for most of that first month, until one day I didn't notice it anymore.

"Anyway, one night, my wife and I went to a big confab on Agent Orange, and this distinguished doctor gave a speech on how it affects the families of 'Nam vets. When he got to the part about the birth defects, and all the spontaneous miscarriages that the wives were having, my wife turned to me with this look of total hatred, as if to say, 'So *that's* what happened to me, you sonovabitch.' Later, when we got home, I tried to tell her how sorry I was, but she didn't want to hear it, man. All she said was—and I'll never forget the voice she said it in—'*I wish you had died over there, motherfucker. I wish you had never come home.*'"

Though the voice in which Jim says this is even and weightless, the words come out like sledgehammers. I search his huge, pale, sulfurous face for some sign of wounded outrage. Hadn't *he*, after all, with his manifold ailments, been every bit as contaminated by it as she, and no less an unwitting victim? But his eyes give out only a bleat of confusion, as if, in the stop-time conflux of guilt and rage, he has no idea *what* to feel anymore.

"What did you say to her?" I ask after a moment.

"Nothing." He shrugs. "What was there to say? I had fucked up her life but good."

ONE OF THE FIRST THINGS THAT STRUCK ME about PTSD was how preternaturally fickle it was. In some men, it struck at the earliest opportunity, cracking them up over the walkout of their girlfriend back home or the wave of abuse at the airport. In others, it lay in wait through setback after setback, only to spring at the unlikeliest occasion. Jim, for example, slogged through two decades of rough strife, losing several good jobs to budget cuts and a number of close buddies to suicide. And yet, after enduring all that and a great deal more with courage and equanimity, never missing a mortgage installment or making his kids do without, he suddenly, precipitously, fell flat on his back when the United States thrashed Iraq in the Gulf War.

"Looking back now, part of [the collapse] had to do with me losing my job [to the military money crunch created by Desert Shield]; I mean, that was the third time in ten years I'd had the rug pulled out from me, and I was *tired* of it, already," he seethes. "But the main thing, the real deal, was all the fucking hoopla going on over those goddamn Desert Storm pukes. Excuse me, but what fucking war were *they* ever in, these little REMF bastards with the sand in their boots and a dumbshit grin on their face. That was such a titanic struggle, *it was over in five days*, and not one of those so-called heroes fired a shot in anger—it was all done for them from planes and rocket launchers. And then they come back here to lovefests and parades, and as part of my new job at Fort Monmouth [New Jersey], I've got to throw a huge victory celebration for 'em, and tie a yellow ribbon around anything that ain't moving, and make every service in the world available to the relatives of these schmucks. *In short, I've gotta do everything for them that wasn't done for us, and we fought our fucking hearts out for this country. . . ."*

By now he is in a ferment and balling his fists, and every square inch of him is moving, roiling. His voice has taken on not its old bellicosity, but something hotter, purer, issuing from his core.

"It was like the whole fucking war was an excuse to rub our faces in it, to show us what *we* could've had if we'd only done our job. In the cafeteria, all these military intelligence punks came up to me and said, 'You fucking guys are a bunch of losers; we won *our* war in a breeze.' *You* did? Excuse me, but you didn't even *go over there*, asshole. You just sat around and watched it on TV, like I did.

"Anyhow, that was it for me, man—it was either get out or kill them with my bare fuckin' hands, so I quit my job, sold everything I had, and spent the next three years falling apart in South Carolina."

It should be noted here that Jim's breakdown was scarcely the only one triggered by Desert Storm. According to the therapists I talked to at the shelter and the VA's Vet Centers, a profusion of Vietnam vets came in off the streets in full crisis mode during the war. So provocative were those pictures beamed back by satellite of night-time bombing runs and mass destruction that even vets already in care were having flashbacks and paranoid delusions that "the Cong were out there again."

But for Jim, what was occasioned was less a reliving of the war than its bleak, untreated aftermath. It came back to him that he'd gone to see his father after 'Nam, expecting that he, at least, would understand what he'd been through. The old man, after all, had fought in a recon unit of the

Eleventh Armored Division and had been wounded severely in the Battle of the Bulge. Though a distant, bitter man who kept the world at arm's length, he'd wept openly when he saw his son off to Vietnam, and told him he was the proudest father on earth that day. But seven months later, when Jim drove down to Waltham to see him, the old man spat and turned his back.

"I'd forgotten how much that hurt till all these years later, but I was really counting on him then," Jim says. "I felt totally alone in the world, everybody else had sold me out—my wife, my buddies from high school, the VFW— and I needed some help from him, man. I was expecting him to throw his arm around my shoulder, and say, 'C'mon, you and me are going for a walk.' For twenty years, I'd had to listen to *his* war stories; now I needed him to listen to mine. But instead, all he said was, 'What the hell's the matter with you, you couldn't beat a bunch of gook farmers? I fought the elite First Waffen, the best troops in the German SS, and I kicked the crap out of 'em, blah blah blah.' He died six years later without ever hearing about my war, and because of that, I didn't feel anything when he croaked. I threw him a huge funeral, brought his whole family up here and everything, even buried him with a bronze plaque in the veterans' section of the cemetery. But the whole thing was totally empty and meaningless for me because he'd betrayed me and deserted me at the time I needed him the most."

In all the years since, nothing has so constrained Jim or kept him at bay as his bitter certainty of betrayal. At the first sign of treachery in people, no matter how slight, he is out the door and down the block before they know what hit them. Like so many Vietnam vets, he has a fierce code of loyalty that virtually no one else can live by. It forgets nothing and forgives nothing and brooks no terms in its division of the world into two camps—the brothers, and everyone else. Its function, of course, is defensive, to protect the organism from further harm. But in its overscrupulous zeal, it keeps out everything else as well, including any intimation of love and sympathy. By leagues or degrees, it closes down the circle, until there is no one left inside it but the self.

THAT IS WHY THE COMBAT SUPPORT GROUP AT the shelter is so important: it opens up the circle once again. Every Tuesday and Thursday evening, in a third-floor room that is about as cheerful as a gas chamber, twenty to thirty Vietnam vets get together to let it all hang out: the war, and everything before and after. The meetings, which go on for two or three hours, can be messy, tearful, bruising affairs— and yet, none of the men who attend them speak of the anguish involved. What they talk about, instead, is *love*.

"I'm closer to every guy in that room upstairs than I am to my own family," says Jim. "That's not to put down either of my kids, who I love a lot and who I'm sure love me, at least most of the time. But these guys are the first people in twenty-seven years who *listened* to me and didn't run away. Who didn't start looking down at their watches, or tapping their feet and saying, 'Jesus Christ, guy, I've gotta get outta here, I'm late.' Not only did these guys not condemn me for 'Nam, they took me into their hearts and kept me there. They said, in so many words, 'We love you, man,' and I'd never even gotten that from any of the vets I've helped.

"Somebody was asking me the other day what that vibe is about, how come us cold, hard dudes are always talking about how we love each other. I told him it comes from having survived two wars together—the war over there and the one back here. I mean, when you've been hounded into your basement by your own fucking people, and made to feel so ashamed of yourself that you lied about who you are, it feels *good*, goddamnit, to be with your brothers, and to let all that vile shit come out of you finally. It feels *good* to find out that you matter to somebody, and they matter to you right back; it'd been so long since I'd had any feelings for anybody, I thought I was fucking dead inside.

"That's the thing about this group that's so different from all the others I've been in. There's a lot of these deals where the focus is on conflict, everyone going after each other about what pisses them off, or what this one over there is trying to hide from everyone else. Here, the whole vibe is about validation, guys telling you over and over that they've been there, too, and are still alive to talk about it. That doesn't mean there's a lot of grab-ass going on, brothers trying to make you feel better with any of that touchy-feely crap. No, believe me, man, the truth is in that room, but a lot of the time it's coming out of somebody else's mouth. When I came in here six months ago and started talking about my guilt, the guys all went around the room talking about theirs. Some of them were suffering because they'd come back without a scratch, and a lot of their buddies were cripples or amputees. Other guys talked about how much it fucked with them that they survived, whereas so many of their brothers came home in a box. And when they came back around to me, they all let me know that I'd done the right thing, that they would've done exactly like I did if they'd gotten the chance to bolt. And for the first time in a real long time, I walked out of there with a little peace. For twenty-seven years, if you could've split me open, you'd've seen like this black space as empty as the Siberian, and a wind howling through there that've snapped your ears shut. That night, the wind stopped blowing as hard, and just about every week since, there's been a little less of it, to the point where I can almost imagine waking up in the morning and hearing nothing but silence in my head.

"Now, I'm not making out like I'm anywhere near there yet. I've still got all that rage and anger inside me, and that's pretty much what I put out when I meet non-vets like you. Stay back. Don't fuck with me. Pissed-off 'Nam vet coming through. But I think what's happening in there is we're teaching each other about human relations again. We're learning that you can be jerked off at a guy and tell him how you feel about it, and you'll both still be alive in the morning. We're learning that you can go ahead and break down and cry in here, or talk about all the things you're ashamed of in yourself, and your business won't be put out onto the street by someone. That's trust, man, or at least the first little bit of it, and you're looking at someone who hasn't trusted another person since 1967. The next step, eventually, is to start trusting someone *outside* the group, but that feels like it's miles away yet. I'm just coming off a thing in South Carolina that knocked me for a two-year loop."

He points toward a picture of a stunning woman on his wall, and from the proud, despondent gaze he casts on it, it is clear that he is still in love with her. "Oh man, it's an old, old story." He sighs. "I fell apart and went down there to be taken care of for a little while, and instead, I wound up taking care of her. Sounds stupid, but I've been doing that for fifteen years, ever since I got involved with veteran activism in the seventies. I was elected the second president of VEVA [Vietnam-Era Veterans Association, an organization of several hundred members in Massachusetts] after the first president blew his head off, and would get calls at all hours of the day and night, telling me to come over ASAP—some Marine'd be sitting in his attic with a .45, getting ready to whack himself out. And I'd run over there and he's drunk as a skunk and beat the shit out of his wife with a broom handle, and I'm telling him, 'Yo, brother, take the clip outta the gun and slide it over; *then*, we can sit down and talk.' And after a while, he'd lay it down, and we'd sit there dealing till sunup, crying and weeping it out until he's back in his right mind. And man, I did this and did this for so many guys, dealing with all of their shit and never dealing with mine, until finally I just crisped and said, I can't take it anymore. I need someone now to catch *my* fall. . . ."

He stops, suspended over a new emotion, a great, beckoning sorrow that he wants no part of. He gets up, almost knocking the chair over in his haste, and goes outside for a smoke, while I sit there much chastened by what it costs these men to talk. Many of them have gone into deep depressions after being interviewed, slipping back into the old chokedamp of night sweats and memories, walking around with the look of the damned. Weeks or months later, having pulled out of it at great anguish, they've come up to me and said, "Hey, dude, thanks a lot for that, man, I needed to go back there again." But this, of course, is bullshit, the butch swagger of a scared grunt. Nobody, no matter how numb or frosty, needs to go back to *that* place again.

Moreover, it is one thing to tell these stories from a safe remove, looking back, after five or ten years to the good, at the horror show that had been your life. But it is quite another when you were living in your car six months ago, inching up the coastline on your last fifty dollars. When Jim pulled in here to apply for work in February, he was subsisting on his $400-a-month war-wounds pension and sleeping on the couch of a friend in Waltham. He'd never applied for PTSD benefits or the Agent Orange money owed him because that would have required that he declare himself disabled, and this he flatly refused to do. Even now, with a job in the shelter's employment office, he is living in a damp, shabby room in Hull and is several years away, at least, from an upgrade in his pension. At 56, he hasn't worked in his field since 1991 and is rarely extended the courtesy of a reply when he sends out his résumé.

But for all that he keeps driving, keeps moving his feet, like a ball carrier who refuses to go down. He is saving up his money and will begin looking for a loft soon, where, with enough space for his easels and a little light in the afternoon, he can finally take up his life's work again. Since the day he came back from Vietnam, he has dreamed of painting a series of large pictures about the war and exhibiting them around the country. Inspired by the firing-squad horror of Goya's work, he has already done the preliminary sketches in his head. In one, he is sitting in full combat gear on the Red Line subway in Boston. It is well after midnight and he is bathed in green light in a car that is empty but for a Viet Cong in the seat beside him. Through the windows can be read the sign of the station they are pulling into. It says *Dao Thien Crossing*, not *Downtown Crossing*, and there is no getting home from there. In another, a beautiful Vietnamese with her back to the viewer is leaning over the rail of a balcony. As seductive as she is bored, she is smoking a cigarette disinterestedly while beneath her stretches a scene of untold carnage: the burned and broken turrets of U.S. tanks, downed choppers, torched villages, and composts of bodies, a garden of earthly affrights. The title of the picture is *Saigon Tea*, as in the leering proposition, "You buy me one Saigon tea, GI?"

"There it is," he says, "all still fucked up inside me—the

sex, the death, the sickness, the excitement—I just can't seem to get away from it, man. But I figure, you know, if I can ever paint it big enough and strong enough, maybe someone out there'll feel what I've been feeling. Maybe their heart'll start beating a little quicker, and their mouth'll go dry, and they'll stare at that goddamn painting trying to figure out what it's doing to 'em, and for that thirty or forty seconds, they'll be where I've been. Whether or not they like it is besides the point. I just want somebody in this fucking country to have an *emotion* about that war, to stand there and feel something other than 'Who cares?' and 'Go away.' If you're gonna send your kids off to a place like this, you better damn well know what they're all coming back with. Otherwise, it really all *was* for nothing, what we went through and what I'll go through till the day I die."

CHAPTER SEVEN

HE CANNOT QUITE PINPOINT WHEN IT HAPPENED, this being twenty-seven years ago. Maybe it was after his unit murdered the old man in the village, slaughtering him like a pig because he couldn't tell them where the Cong were. Or maybe it was the day he lost his buddy Michael in action, a hurt so deep it still shortens his breath, jabbing him like a K-bar between the ribs. But whatever it was that finally pushed him over the top, nothing on earth was going to make him back down. Six months into his tour in Vietnam, Richie Haudel decided that he wasn't going to fight anymore, or do anything else to aid and abet the effort in War Zone C. He has, to put this as delicately as possible, been paying for it in blood ever since.

It must be understood that we are not talking about a coward here, or about a belated pacifist whose qualms caught up to him. Haudel was a hard-eyed kid who'd been in and out of reform school since 15, and who went over in 1966 with arguably the roughest crew in III Corps, the 173rd Airborne. He was a wild man on slack time, disobeying orders and hanging AWOL, but in combat was so locked in that they kept him out there on the point, carving out a path for them through the sucking, poisoned jungle. Just before he quit, in fact, he'd been put in for a Bronze and for his second Purple Heart with oak leaf cluster.

Nevertheless, the day they drove him to the stockade in Long Binh, he told the C.O. there what he'd told his lieutenant, that he not only refused to bear arms anymore, he also declined to salute and make reveille.

"Oh, is that so?" said the captain, a slab-shouldered lifer in the military police. "Well, as it happens, we've got just the place for you."

They stripped him to his shorts and marched him out of the stockade to a series of steel boxes set off in a clearing. The boxes, called Conex containers, had been used to transport cargo and were nothing more than narrow crates with slats cut lengthwise for air. They threw him into one of these with a half-canteen of water and kept him sealed up there for better than ten days. By mid-morning, the heat inside the box was such that he was already delirious with thirst and fever, calling upon God and his long-dead grandmother to bear him up through this hell.

"It wasn't nothing more than a microwave in there—the whole idea of it was to break my will," says Haudel. "At night, they dragged me out to where nobody could hear it and beat me up good with air hoses, this big, huge sergeant and his MP stooges. To eat, all I got was three crusts of bread, and on the fourth day, a plate of lettuce and cucumbers. But I wasn't gonna crack out there 'cause I had made this commitment, and I'd rather have died than broke it. I wasn't real religious yet—that came years and years later, in Charles Street prison—but I knew the difference between good and evil. My whole tour, we were goin' into villes and finding no trace of the VC anywhere, but burning 'em down anyway 'cause Army intelligence said they were hostile.

And we'd do it right in fronta those people, with all their women and kids cryin', and if we received even one round of sniper fire, we'd call in the planes and heavy artillery and waste everybody in there.

"For a while, I managed to shut down, just watched it but felt nothing; said, fuck it, man, that's war. These people asked for it. But after month after month of this, watching innocent people die without no justification for it, the rage and anger built up to where it turned against myself. The whole world was upside down, everything I believed in was wrong—good was evil, evil was good, I was lost in a counterfeit universe. The only way to stop it was to say, *Stop*, no more. And once I did that, there was no going back on it."

On his tenth day in the box, Haudel was carted out on a stretcher and brought, near death, to a tent in the stockade. For days, they pumped him full of food and fluids, then asked him, when he was upright again, if he had changed his mind. No, he replied, I will not serve, and so they handcuffed him once more and dragged him out to the container, where he lasted two weeks this stint. Five times they took him out to roast in the Conex, and five times he came back delirious but unbroken. The last time, however, they switched him over to solitary in the compound, a tight, soundproof cell kept in perfect darkness. There, deprived of light and noise, he finally, inevitably fell apart, and banged on the door wildly, begging the captain for mercy.

"They opened up the door and there he was, all smiles, so happy to see he'd finally broke me," says Haudel. "He literally made me get down on my hands and knees and kiss his fucking boots, and I did it, man. I did it and I cried and cried and cried, because now I had nothing left—no

God, no country, no will, no nothing. I was totally empty, totally destroyed. They put me in general confinement and kept me there for two more weeks, then sent me back home on a plane, in handcuffs.

"But right before they released me, they sent someone in to see me, the highest-ranking NCO in the United States Army. He was the brigade command sergeant major, a Congressional Medal of Honor winner and a World War II hero, and he sat down and talked to me like a father would to a son. He said he knew who I was and why I'd did what I did, and that he had the greatest respect and admiration for me, but that it was his duty to tell me what was gonna happen to me if I didn't change my mind. If I *did* change it, he said, he'd give me any job I wanted. I could drive a jeep for the colonel and not haveta fight, just do my six months there and get out. But if I didn't change my mind, they would dishonor, discredit, and discharge me, and I would regret it for the rest of my life. I said, 'Then so be it, sir. I've made my decision. I can't go against what I know is wrong and evil.'"

Three days later, when he landed in Oakland, Haudel found the sergeant major as good as his word. By law, Richie couldn't be court-martialed for refusing to fight (in the stockade, he had applied for conscientious-objector status), so, instead, the Army drummed him out for refusing to get a haircut and for possession of a single joint of marijuana. He was given an undesirable discharge, stripped of his rank and all his medals, and cashiered without a dime of the combat pay owed him. And, in its consummate expression of martial loathing, the Army even contrived to lose his records, effectively telling him and anyone else who asked: Richard Morgan Haudel never happened.

*   *   *

OF ALL THE SUNDRY OUTRAGES OF THE WAR IN Vietnam (and have any other *five* wars yielded as many?), few are as sad and insupportable as the fate of the men with bad discharges. According to Bob Sinclair, a national service officer at the DAV, "there are tens of thousands of combat vets with bad paper from that war. That means they got no medical benefits for their injuries, they couldn't apply for VA disability, or get into a state program for PTSD. Some of them, of course, were discharged for legitimate reasons— striking an officer, for example, or breaking and entering. But with the great majority of them, I would say, it was nickel-and-dime stuff, like insubordination, or getting drunk and staying out AWOL for a day.

"What happened in so many of these cases is you had a guy came back from 'Nam with some time left on his tour, and emotionally, he couldn't make the adjustment to garrison duty," says Sinclair, a former recon trooper in the Eleventh Armored Cav who has three Purple Hearts to his credit. "Maybe a month or so earlier, they'd been out on search-and-destroy, killing or being killed in the Ashau Valley. Now, all of a sudden, they've got to make reveille at Fort Hood, Texas, and stand there at attention all day with spit-shined boots, and take orders from NCOs who hadn't even *been* to 'Nam. A lot of guys couldn't handle that, they needed months to decompress, and it was only a matter of when, not if, they went over the line. But when you think about it, isn't it mind-blowing that they survived Vietnam, fighting for their country with valor and distinction, and then got bounced for some infraction back home? To me, that's just a real hard pill to swallow."

Multipy that indignation by a factor of ten, and you will arrive at some small idea of Haudel's rage. Among even the pugs and street vets of South Boston, he was legendary, a demon, sending out hate so irradiated they could practically see him in the dark. Almost 50 now and shattered by a life in the gutter (recent X rays revealed that, at one time or another, virtually every major bone in his body has been broken), he nevertheless has one of those faces you wouldn't dream of crossing. Becalmed a bit after eight months of intensive therapy at the shelter, it heats up again in a heartbeat when you raise the subject of bad paper. His skin, already ruddy from the residue of dioxin, turns the virulent purple of an hour-old bruise, and his eyes come at you like rounds of white phosphorous, devouring all the oxygen in the room.

"If anyone in this fuckin' place deserves one hundred percent [PTSD disability pension], it's guys like [fellow shelter vets] Al Brown and Harvey Metcalf, who's dying from Agent Orange poisoning," he grunts, grinding his jaws. "And yeah, as far as it goes, I shoulda gotten it, too, because I gave those cocksuckers everything I had over there, and they took it from me and didn't even give me the fuckin' medals I'd earned. [After a fifteen-year paper duel with the VA, Haudel has finally received a partial list of his decorations.] What they didn't do to me in the bush, they did in that goddamn container, torturin' me and beatin' me like I was some kinda animal. I met a lotta guys in Walpole [State Penitentiary] with some of the same problems, and it made me even angrier to see how many of us they'd screwed. I'm not sayin' I was an angel in 'Nam, but I damn sure did more in those first six months than a lotta guys I know gettin' [PTSD] pensions."

He comes up for air a moment, then pushes off again, inveighing against the liars and psychopaths he's met who have scammed the VA for millions. In his zero-sum arithmetic, every dollar paid out to a "wannabe vet" (a rear-echelon type posing as a fried line grunt) deprives Haudel and men like him of their rightful due. In his long and bitter passage through the bowels of the system—the drunk tanks and Vet Centers and support groups in prison—he has met dozens of these so-called wannabe vets and has come to despise every aspect of their nature. With their lies and loquacity and can-you-top-this war stories, they destroy "every goddamn thing they get their hands on," he says, particularly the morale of the "true brothers who come together to heal."

But spend an hour or two with Haudel and you see that behind the gruff manner and the battered club-fighter's face, there is something remarkably pure about him, a kind of childlike capacity for love and pleasure. It survived somehow his abandonment, at the age of three, by both his parents, and the subsequent, daily sadism of his foster father, who beat him up so badly that he had to run away to save his life. It survived the torture, in captivity, of those six months in Long Binh and comparable stretches of solitary confinement in the state pens at Walpole and Concord, sleeping on filthy, shit-stained mattresses in rooms no bigger than that steel box.

But even more remarkably, it survived twenty-seven years of complete sensory deprivation, twenty-seven years without love or sex or incidental human contact. So disaccustomed, in fact, was Richie to the sensation of being touched, that when he fell in love last spring with a young nurse at a city hospital, he had literally to be taught to put his arms around her, and not to panic when she did likewise. In this shelter, where the miraculous is practically commonplace, nothing quite compares to the brief romance of Richie and Lisa, but in order to properly appreciate it, you must first understand how far he had fallen.

*   *   *

IF YOU LIVE IN A CITY OF ANY SIZE IN THIS COUN-
try, you will doubtless have seen someone resembling
Richie at low ebb. As recently as last winter, he was one of
those drunks on the sidewalk in the knocked-stiff contortion
of the dead. Caked for weeks in his own waste and spotted
with lesions the size of golf balls, the edema of a massive
staph infection, he was most conspicuous for the many
scabs on his face, some no older than a few hours. (How,
you may have asked yourself, stepping over somebody like
him, could anyone so enfeebled have been in so many
fights? Answer: He probably wasn't; he cut himself trying to
stand up; the first thing to go in a career drinker is his equi-
librium.)

In fact, when Haudel was wheeled into Boston City
Hospital in December, he likely had no more than a day or
two to live. Aside from the raging staph infection, he was
suffering from a case of acute blood poisoning and would
doubtless have died in a matter of hours without an infusion
of antibiotics. Two weeks later, when he was out of the
woods, they sent him across town to a place called The
Respite, a superb convalescent unit where Lisa happened to
work. Richie had been admitted there six months earlier (a
broken shoulder and three fractured ribs that trip) but was
totally insensible of her interest in him. ("How," he asks now,
"was I supposed to pick up on that—this beautiful, young
girl, who in her spare time is an artist and a ballet dancer,
wanting anything to do with a bum like me?") Even after he
was discharged in September and Lisa roamed the bars of
Southey looking for him, finally finding him in an above-
ground subway shack and buying him a pair of warm boots
for the winter—even then, he didn't catch on to the obvious,
that she loved him and was determined to save him.

"What I saw in Richie—what a *lot* of us [at The Respite] saw in Richie—was this gentleness and decency underneath the pain," says Lisa, whom Richie brings over for dinner one night, holding her hand shyly under the table. She is a tall, pretty woman with a sweet sprawl of curls, and gray eyes of such directness you feel you've known her since childhood. "The way he took care of all the flowers there, and tried to cheer *us* up, instead of the other way around— it was just obvious to me that this was a real special person here. The problem, though, was that he had no hope, no will. He wanted to stop drinking, but it never lasted for him because of the war stuff, and he was convinced he was going to die soon and there was nothing anyone could do to stop it."

"That's true," Richie puts in. "The last time I'd stopped drinkin' was back in '87, and the depression that came over me then was worse than anything you can ever imagine. At the time, I had some money from my Agent Orange settlement and was livin' in a little studio over in Waltham. I made two and a half years of sobriety, but I might as well have been in the Hole in Walpole—I was in solitary inside my head. In fact, it wasn't till I went to a hospital in Jamaica Plain last February and found out about dual-diagnosis that a light went on inside my head. All these years, I'd been goin' to Bridgewater [State Hospital] to dry out, but nobody would touch my PTSD, or I'd do a program at Rutland Heights but it didn't deal with the alcoholism, and I'd go right back out to Southey and pick up all over again. When I got outta that hospital in JP and came to the shelter in March, I knew that, either way, this was the last stop on the line for me. Either it was gonna click with George [Mendoza] and the group, or I was a fuckin' dead man; there was no way I was gonna survive another trip on the streets."

For all that, he was highly skeptical when he joined the group in March. He'd been in plenty of these things before, had even started one up in prison, and been burned by it every time, hating himself for having hoped again. But straightaway, he was struck by the differences here. For one thing, there was the group's vast respect for Mendoza, who presided over the meetings like a benevolent rabbi, saying little but infusing everyone with his calm and sympathy. For another, there was something spiritual in the air, all the brothers bearing witness to one another's suffering instead of competing with, or trying to discredit it. In the other groups Haudel had joined, a kind of war had broken out, splinter sects forming according to rank or service, or who the *real* bad mothers had been. In this room, no one seemed to care about any of that crap. What counted, instead, was humility, and a sense of awe at the task before them.

"One of the first things George puts out there is that we were *all* morally annihilated in 'Nam," says Peace Foxx, one of the founders of the shelter and a charter member of the PTSD group. "We *all* went up against absolute evil there, and we *all* made the same basic moral decision—to join the evil and survive, instead of resist it and die. And because we were all soldiers, we've always dealt with that guilt alone. 'It's *my* problem, *I'll* handle it. Go away and leave me alone, man.' What George does is to get us to turn that over to the group, to trust our brothers in there with that pain and that misery, and to bless each other with some forgiveness. Not everyone in there is religious, or prays to the same God. But the spirit of God is most definitely in there, and that's the power of unconditional love."

"Yes, it is," murmurs Richie, glaring at me for emphasis. "Ever since I come home from Vietnam, I'd been in constant spiritual conflict with God. I used'ta curse Him, blame Him for all the things that happened to me there, and all the evil I witnessed that He allowed to exist. In San Francisco, I made a deal with Him after I stabbed somebody almost to death. I said, 'God, I promise I won't hurt no one else if you just leave me the fuck alone. Just forget about me and let me go drink in peace,' and He did, and that's all I did for thirteen years.

"But by '81 I found I couldn't go on no more. I desperately needed help and was turnt away everywhere I went for it, and I had just robbed three banks to try and get someone to listen to me. I was in Station Four in the South End, in a dirty, freezing jail cell without no jacket on 'cause the cops had stolen it, and I dropped to my knees and surrendered to God. I just broke down and cried and said, 'Please, please help me, God. You killed me in Vietnam, and I've been dead ever since, but I wanna try and live again. How do I do it, how do I come back to life, and how long is it gonna take me?' *'Thirteen years,'* He told me, and don't ask me how He told me, but that was what He said. Thirteen more years of pain and suffering, He said, but now there was a purpose to it. Now, it was gonna be my job to be a *witness*, to watch and to learn what was being done to my brothers. Because, when they sent me up to Walpole after the trial, I was in for the fuckin' shock of my life—the place was just *crawlin'* with Vietnam combat vets. I'm tellin' you, we had our own *units* in there, is how many of us they had locked up, around thirty percent of the overall prison population. And a lot of 'em were ravin' lunatics, too, guys totally gone and livin' in their own worlds, and insteada tryin' to do something to help 'em, the shrinks were shovin' fistfuls of shit down their throats—Elavil, Stelazine, Thorazine, Haldol. I was so bullshit over our treatment, I joined a group called AVIP (American Veterans in Prison) to try and get some kinda decent therapy for the brothers. Thanks to a wonderful, sweet lady named Sarah Haley [a clinical social worker with the VA], who took down my whole history and explained to me about PTSD, I finally knew a little bit about what we were all suffering from, but nowhere could I get ahold of somebody in power who gave like even half a shit."

Indeed, so galled was he by the public's indifference that when he was released in 1984, he robbed a bank to protest it, running out into the street and throwing all the money in the air. Possessed of neither a gun nor a getaway car, he was picked up almost immediately for the heist, and, owing to a declaration of war that he'd mailed to the *Herald*, was tried with much fanfare the following fall. State veterans groups, eager to mount a test case for the PTSD defense, offered him top-dollar legal assistance if he agreed to a diminished-capacity plea. True to form, Richie told them all to go fuck themselves and stood up in open court to explain what he'd done:

"My combat brothers and I were destroyed by what we did in Vietnam, murderin' and slaughterin' innocent people who were livin' in the Stone Age, and now we're bein' destroyed all over again right here," he said. "We're bein' caged up in solitary, or sent to hospitals for the criminally insane, sittin' there for months and years in a filthy room with no window, listenin' all day and night to the screams of the lunatics. We're bein' beaten up by the guards there, who are sicker than any of the inmates, and walkin' into bathrooms where crazy men are committing oral sex on each other, and fillin' up soda cans with their own feces and urine and drinkin' it right in front of us.

"The reason I'm here today is because I deliberately did a crime, to bring attention to what's happenin' to Vietnam vets behind bars. I had no weapon on me whatsoever when I did the crime, and I threw all the money in the street, because what I did that day wasn't about keepin' the money. I did it because I truly believed that the news media would help us, which they haven't. I truly believed the veterans groups would help us, which they haven't. I'm not sayin' what I did was right, but I didn't know what else to do. Somehow, somebody out there hadda listen to our story."

As he remembers it, the jury deliberated for exactly forty-five minutes before finding him guilty of armed robbery. Two weeks later, at sentencing, however, their verdict was essentially overturned. Clearly moved by Richie's statement, the judge sentenced him not to life imprisonment (this was Haudel's third felony conviction) but to the rock-bottom minimum, two years plus time served. In his cell that night, Richie got down on his knees and thanked God. Somehow, somebody out there *had* listened to his story, had heard, beyond the charges, the voice of grief and agony speak, and had responded with a measure of condolent mercy.

"The judge that day gave me back what the Army took away, my sense of honor and integrity," says Richie. "I knew then that I was right, what I'd did in Vietnam, and that all those years of pain and suffering were worth it. And I knew then that it was also right, what I had done in that bank. Someone hadda stand up and say, 'No more of this, already. We're human beings, not animals, and you can't keep fuckin' treatin' us this way."

Richie went back to prison and did the rest of his time wisely, studying for—and earning—his General Equivalency Degree (he had an eighth-grade education when he was sent to Vietnam). And, after being paroled in 1988, he did two long stints at a PTSD program, trying to untie the blood-knot of his anger. He could feel it in his chest, he says, a fist right next to his heart, and in the morning when he woke up, the hate would rush to his head, an overwhelming impulse to hurt someone, to strike out blindly at the world. He got deeply involved with AA, then dropped it abruptly; read his Bible devoutly, but got no peace from it. Hopeless and heart-broken, he slid back into the streets, waiting out the inevitable, a cold death in someone's doorway.

"I'd given up, like Lisa told you; I just wanted it to be over with," he says. "All my life, you know, I'd always did everything alone. I lived alone, I did time alone, I slept alone, and I drank alone, and now all I wanted to do was just die alone. But Lisa wouldn't let me, she kept poppin' up lookin' for me, trudgin' through alla that snow last winter to bring me food and clothes, or takin' me back to her place to clean me up, give me a hot bath. And my first day at the shelter, she was with me then, too, meetin' George and Tommy Connally, and alla the other brothers in the group. It was real rough on me for a while there, bein' so used to total isolation, and havin' to live all of a sudden among three hundred men, and tolerate the screws [security guards] without goin' bullshit on them.

"But Lisa kept comin' to see me, takin' me out to dinner or back over to her place, and little by little—I couldn't stop myself—I found myself totally in love with her. In fact, the night it finally happened and we went to bed together, I was so stunned and bedazzled afterwards that I walked three miles in the wrong direction for the subway. I couldn't believe that God had sent me someone like her, so beautiful and so loving and doesn't have a mean bone in her body. We don't have anything in common—she eats organic food, and I can't stand the crap; she likes crazy music, I like classical. And, thanks to George and the group, I'm changin' so fast now that I don't know how it's gonna work out with her. She's used to the drunk, helpless bastard who came in here eight months ago, and that ain't me anymore. I don't know *who* I am half the time, but I finally got me a little peace, and ain't nothin' and no one gettin' in the way of that. I keep tellin' her straight out, that group is number one in my life, and everything else is a distant second. She doesn't like hearin' that, but the truth is all I got, and the truth is I'm totally dedicated to helpin' George and the brothers."

To that end, he recently broke up with Lisa, and has become a full-time volunteer in Mendoza's office, answering the phones and escorting the new guys to their medical appointments. He moved out of the shelter recently to a room at the Y, where he spends his evenings reading the Bible and world theology. He lives on a small stipend from Social Security, and has begun the long process of filing for an upgrade of his discharge, which would entitle him, if successful, to apply for PTSD benefits.

"It ain't about the money," he grunts. "I already give away what little I got—two bucks here, three bucks there to guys I see on the street, and believe me, *I* know the ones who need it and who don't. No, I want it from 'em to recognize that damage was done, that my *soul* was murdered three times over by what they did to me. I'm still fightin' it every day, the rage and the anger that's still down there inside a' me, and that'll probably always go on bein' there, ready to blow. But right now, the good in me is winnin' out over the evil, and for the first time in a long time, I'm not hurtin' anyone, includin' myself. That's what all of us got in common, you know, besides the war—a dark fuckin' evil that doesn't go away. All I can do is say no to it, a day at a time, and keep prayin' that one day it'll be easier for me than it is right now."

*   *   *

SIX-FIFTEEN ON A DAMP EVENING IN OCTOBER, and almost thirty of us are packed into this long flowerbox of an office. The Thursday night meeting of the combat support group hasn't even begun yet, and already the air is unbreathable for smoke, a cigarette burning in every mouth or hand, like citronella to ward off mosquitoes. On many of these faces are writ the sad residuum of that war: the telltale acne of Agent Orange; the scars and smashed noses of knife fights and bar brawls. And yet, something else is manifest here besides smoke and pregame jitters, a perspicuous pleasure at being together again. I hear parts of a dozen brisk conversations and the sort of bloody insults only true friends would brazen. Were it not for all the gung-ho decorations in the room—the flags and SEMPER FI signs and camouflage curtains—we could just as easily be sitting in someone's den, or at the counter in a bowling alley.

At 6:30, Mendoza calls the meeting to order. Gravely elegant in a striped tie and charcoal cardigan, his silver hair swept off his nut-brown forehead, he tells the brothers that the last couple of sessions have been dark—very dark—and for that reason, he would like to talk about healing tonight. What *is* healing, anyway, he asks the group. What does it feel like, what does it look like—and when, if ever, did it begin for you?

An uneasy, swivel-headed silence goes around, and then a guy with orange hair and exhausted eyes speaks up. "Hi, I'm Mike, I was a two-tour medic in 'Nam, and tonight is my first night in the group with you guys—"

"*Welcome home, brother,*" comes the response from around the room. "Glad you made it back, bro."

"Thank you all," says Mike, both touched and rattled. "I—I wouldn't say I was home yet, but I'm in a lot better place than I was ten days ago, sleeping on the sidewalk and eating out of a Dumpster. I just want to say I don't know what healing is, or if I even deserve it, but I think I maybe got a little bit of it the other day, when the Gold Star moms [mothers of dead Vietnam vets] were downstairs [for a benefit]. In my two tours in the Delta, I put at least a couple of hundred kids into body bags, and I know what their last moments alive were like. No matter what lies I told them, almost all of them knew they were dying, and they were scared shit and calling out for their mothers to help them— some of 'em were in so much pain, in fact, they thought *I* was their mother, and I'd let 'em hold my hand and go on thinking that until we got back to the evac.

"Well, Sunday night, I got to tell one of those women something that I think mighta really helped her, which is that, regardless of who her son was or how he died, I knew that his final thoughts had been with her. She hugged me when she heard that, and thanked me a lot, and I felt like, finally, maybe I had given some comfort to someone, which is kinda why I became a medic in the first place.

"Now, I'm not gonna lie to you guys, I'm scared like a motherfuck of this place. I've walked into this building before, took one look around me, and got the hell out of here as fast as I could—I just wasn't ready to do the work. I *still* don't know if I can handle what's coming, but I do know that I'm forty-four and I've got three kids I love, and the easy way out for me stopped being easy a long time ago."

The brothers barrage him with pledges of support and imprecations to just "be there," to "keep showing up and it'll get better." Jim F., the massive tank commander, takes the floor and testifies. "Healing happens every time I walk through that door, Mike. On our own, we're all struggling with some hard-core demons, but what comes out of us when we're together is this great compassion and spirituality. And I know it ain't comin' from me, brother, 'cause I'm the most godless motherfucker you ever met, but I can tell you this much right now—it's changing me, day by day. This morning, for instance, one of the idiots on the first floor [a staff member] came up and dissed me something fierce. No rhyme, no reason, just jumped in my shit with both shoes on. And instead of doing what I used'ta do, which is break the bastard in half and hide the pieces, I just laughed at him and said, 'Yeah, later, dude,' and carried on with my day.

"See, healing for me is about having *control*, the ability to pick my time and my place. Life sucked when all I did was go to war or hide in the basement. I feel like, finally, I'm startin' to understand how other people live, and I tell you what, man, it feels *good* as hell."

Rob M., a former recon killer in the mountains of Pleiku and Kontum, goes next.

"Mike, I just want to make sure that you got the message—you *are* home, in this room. From now on, this is your clubhouse, your base camp, whatever—you're welcome here anytime. There's always a bunch of us up here, drinking coffee and hanging out, so don't go away feelin' like you gotta hide under a rock the rest of the week. Monday through Friday, this is *your* house, from seven o'clock in the morning.

"Anyway, for me," he continues, "healing is about lettin' myself have feelings again, after twenty-five years of being a walkin' ice cube. I've never been married, and never been able to keep a girlfriend—I just took a hostage every couple of months, you know what I mean? My parents'd written me off, I was livin' out of my car, which was unregistered, and suckin' on that glass dick [a crack pipe] twenty-four/seven. Now, because of all of these guys, and because of that man [Mendoza], who I love dearly, I'm startin' to have feelings again, at least in this room. I don't know where it's goin' yet, or if I'll be able to have feelings for someone outside a' here anytime soon, but for once, I'm allowin' myself to hope a little. You know, I want what everybody else in this world wants—a nice place to live, a woman who loves me, maybe even a kid or two down the road. But for now, I'm right here, where I belong, with my brothers, and that's good enough to do me till I'm ready."

And so on it goes, around the room. Richie Haudel describes a life that looked like "a B-52 had hit it—burnt fields, black smoke, no oxygen in your lungs." And then he found God in jail, and some grace and forgiveness in here, and learned from George that peace came from "being a decent person every day—bringin' a brother over to the hospital, or takin' a new guy under my wing." Chuck Stransky, the Broadway actor, talks about conquering his "terminal uniqueness," the sense of entitlement that comes from "feeling that no one else on earth had ever gone through the things that I had." Jimmy S., who, like Mike, is both a newcomer and a former medic, says that for twenty years, "using [heroin] covered up all of my defects, and let me hide myself away from my family. Being here tonight, I feel some of the faith that I lost when I was in 'Nam. God sent me to this place two weeks ago, and I thank Him from the bottom of my heart for it."

And then, when everybody in the room has said his piece, and offered up his profuse praise to Mendoza, he clears his throat and, damp eyes sparkling, firmly declines any credit. "I am flattered by you guys, but, you know, you're totally, totally wrong—*you* are the ones doing the miracle," he says in his earthy Argentine burr. "*You* are the ones reaching out for the truth, because warriors *need* the truth in order to move, to lead. You are talking always in here about how dark you are, but to me, how I see it, you are full of light, the light that comes from honor. People who have never suffered are empty and do not interest me, whereas you guys have huge hearts and unbelievable spirits. I am asking you to look at yourselves with better eyes, because you are the best of the best, the conscience of your generation. I trust you all with my life, and am so proud to be here tonight."

There is a moment's stunned silence; no one knows quite what to say to this. And then someone in the back calls out, "Give that man a hug," and all at once, they come forward, lurching on sore legs, their arms out to embrace him and to embrace one another, fumbling together in the middle of the room.

EPILOGUE

IT HAS BEEN EIGHTEEN MONTHS SINCE I FIRST SET foot in this shelter, and so much has happened in that time. The staff has grown from 70 to 130, including six new social workers, four job training instructors, and two financial assistance counselors. Construction has been completed on the splendid second-floor barracks and begun on the sixty SRO units on the fifth through seventh floors, for those vets in need of long-term treatment. Across town, sites are being assessed for eighty additional SROs, to be built on a $5 million grant from HUD. (Says Mark Helberg about that grant, and the one for $4.2 million before it: "Thank you, Joe Kennedy II and [Congressman] Joe Moakley and [Governor] Bill Weld, three of the best friends that homeless veterans ever had.")

The list goes on: much of the fourth floor has been converted into classrooms, where hundreds of homeless vets are being trained for jobs as bus drivers, security guards, line cooks, and computer repairmen. And perhaps most significantly, Mendoza's PTSD program has more than tripled in size, as word gets around the Northeast corridor that *this* is where you come for relief from that war.

So much has been done, in other words, but so much remains to be done. There are, by the VA's estimate, almost half a million vets acutely ill with PTSD and doubtless hundreds of thousands more who, out of fear or infirmity, have yet to come in and be counted. There are (again, by VA estimate) a quarter of a million vets sick and hungry on our streets, at least a third of them Vietnam vets. Where are they to turn now for refuge and treatment? To the Dickensian public men's shelters, teeming with thieves and TB? To the VA's psychiatric wards, where they are weaned of booze and street drugs only to be put on psychotropics and sit around in robotic stupors for six months? Remember, these are men who are homeless not because they are lazy or unlucky, but because *they had the guts to stand up for their country when called*. Is this how we wish to reward them for their bravery? Is this what we wish to tell our future defenders, that they have, besides death and maiming to fear, a life in the gutter, despised and cast out?

For almost thirty years, we have been passing around the blame for Vietnam, largely, it seems to me, because no one ever took responsibility for that war. Not one of the three presidents who fomented or fought it had the courage or political clarity to provide a cogent reason for doing so. Most of the blame, consequently, has fallen on those least culpable, namely the three million Americans who served in Southeast Asia between 1965 and 1973. In effect, those kids came home doubly damned, made to bear both the psychic *and* moral curse of Vietnam. For their sins, they ceased being sons and soldiers and became something less than human to us—monsters, baby-killers. Whatever other lessons we may have drawn from that war, we seem to have learned nothing about losing with dignity. It is easy to be gracious when you have all the guns. It is in defeat, however, that you find out what kind of mettle you have. If Vietnam was a referendum on character, we failed, and have not exactly covered ourselves in glory since.

Largely for that reason, the Vietnam War goes on, and will continue to until we decide to stop fixing blame for it, and begin instead to assume *responsibility* for it. What is needed, first of all, is a shelter the size and scale of Court Street in a dozen major cities across the country: New York, Los Angeles, Miami, Washington, Dallas, Detroit, etc. Like Court Street, these should be run not by the mandarins of the VA, but by the grunts and buck sergeants who actually *fought* that war and who are rabidly committed to the welfare of their brothers. Where PTSD and veteran homelessness are concerned, we have tried the conventional methods and failed, just as we tried and failed with conventional warfare in Vietnam. It is time to turn the job over to the Ken Smiths and Mark Helbergs and Peace Foxxes and George Mendozas, who understand in the most visceral way what heals broken vets: the powerful, loving community of peers.

What is needed next, beyond shelters, is transitional housing for these men, affordable SRO units run by and for, again, fellow vets. It avails you nothing to get a homeless Marine back on his feet, then send him to some rooming house to live with drunks and crackheads. Yes, it will cost money to convert abandoned government buildings into safe, clean quarters for recovering vets, but remember, these are, for the most part, men with good jobs who will be *contributing* to the tax base, not perpetually depleting it. Understand also that it is vastly cheaper to help them on the path to independence than it is to abandon them to the mercies of the marketplace. Ken Smith estimates that it costs him $12,000 to rehab a homeless vet and another $3,000 to support him in transitional housing for six months. But it costs the city of Boston almost $20,000 to keep him in a public men's shelter for a year and about $40,000 to lock him up in county jail or a state mental hospital. Says Smith, "Forget, for half a second, this country's debt to these guys, after ripping off the roof of their souls in that war. It just makes good *business sense* to invest in vets, they're about the hardest-working, true-blue people you can hire. Plus, it would save you the trouble of having to step over 'em in the street. Just ask the coroner next January or February how many guys show up on his table with USMC tattooed on their shoulder."

At Fort Ord and Parris Island, it is the first sacrament of honor that Americans go back for their wounded. We pay any price, bear any burden, to bring our brothers in from the field. If those words are to mean anything, we must go back for our wounded, and bring all of them home this time.

HELPING THE SHELTER

THOUGH IT RECEIVES A MODICUM OF MONEY FROM state and local governments, the New England Shelter for Homeless Veterans survives in large part on private donations. If you would like to make a gift to the shelter, write the New England Shelter for Homeless Veterans, Department D, 17 Court Street, Boston, MA 02108, or call (617) 248-9400.

In addition, Leslie Lightfoot has opened a hospice for homeless veterans. It is a fledgling, twelve-bed operation devoted to veterans dying on the street from AIDS. If you would like to support her work, write Veteran Hospice Homestead, 226 Main Street, Leominster, MA 01453, or call (508) 537-7202.